BRAIN STATIONS

BRAIN STATIONS

A CENTER APPROACH TO THINKING SKILLS

By Greta Rasmussen

ISBN 0-936110-07-4
Library of Congress Catalog Card Number: 88-090500
Copyright 1989 by Greta Rasmussen
All rights reserved Printed in the U.S.A.
10 9 8 7 6 5 4 3

TIN MAN PRESS
BOX 219
STANWOOD, WA 98292

Contents

Introduction

Most educators agree that the development of thinking skills among children who will be living their lives in the 21st Century is of critical importance. Knowledge is exploding. So are problems. The ability to bring information into some kind of creative, logical focus is becoming more and more vital. This means that we must produce better thinkers.

But how? How do you teach a child to think? It seems there are as many answers to that question, from our late 20th Century perspective, as there are dedicated and thoughtful people exploring it. That is well and good, for this kind of attention from a variety of viewpoints signals an important beginning.

This book will not add anything to the *theory* of the teaching of thinking skills. That is not its purpose. This book is simply a recognition of one fundamental idea: If you want to teach a child to think, you must first convince that child that thinking is fun and worthwhile.

The central thrust of this book, therefore, is motivational. It is designed to make clear to your students that you, the teacher, hold the process of thinking in high esteem, and that you want to pass along this valuable process to your students.

It is our belief that all children can be taught to think more imaginatively, flexibly and analytically. Obviously, some children are more adept at the process than others, just as some children are more natural artists or athletes. But *all* children, we feel, come with impressive thinking potential as part of their standard equipment, to borrow a phrase from the automakers. All too often, unfortunately, this potential is not realized. It is not our business to examine the complicated reasons why some children turn off and others turn on to the joy of thinking. It is, however, our business to try to "hook" them before the powerful anti-thinking forces in our contemporary society get too strong a grip.

This book, which we call "Brain Stations," is an effort to encourage children to have good experiences in the discipline of thinking. We want them to get the idea at an early age that thinking is fun, that (though it might not be up there with recess) it is important and rewarding. That is why we have chosen the learning center format. To place one child in front of an activity which you, the teacher, have taken time to make, tells that child that he or she is being asked to do something of value.

Now, a word about the nuts and bolts of this book.

You will notice that we have taken pains to vary the texture of the activities in this book. You'll find everything from abstractions to art, from manipulative problems to creative writing. You can contribute to this interest by making the centers yourself. Why? Because youngsters get tired of the sameness of worksheets, and the look-alike quality of commercially prepared graphics. Your hand, your personality, your touch, is more persuasive than you think. Use these things! In other words, have some fun preparing these centers. So what if your lettering is a little shaky and your art is not Rembrandt? Do it! Children will recognize, and respond to, your efforts.

Another note: Since you will be asking children to go individually to a center to "think" about something, you must try to give them (despite your busy schedule) some response. In every case, you'll notice that children are required to turn something in to you. Give them some feedback. Furthermore, when you get some sparks that really light things up (and you will), make a fuss about it. Commend the child and share the accomplishment with the class. (After all, athletic coaches get a lot of mileage out of that approach, don't they?)

So here they are...50 "Brain Stations"...50 thinking centers which will motivate and challenge your students...50 stops along an exciting thinking track. All aboard!

If You Think of...

About this center...

Emphasis here is on flexible thinking. The idea that the same symbol can represent different things depending on the context is not an easy premise, but once children make the connection, they'll be off and running.

Materials needed...

Nine note cards, tagboard.

Directions to students...

Number your paper 1-14, and answer these questions.

If you think of...

1. Number 3 as a nail, what could Number 8 be?

2. Number 4 as a net, what could Number 2 be?

3. Number 1 as snow, what could Number 3 be?

4. Number 7 as a head, what could Number 6 be?

5. Number 1 as eyes, what could Number 9 be?

6. Number 2 as an ant, what could Number 7 be?

7. Number 8 as a lamp, what could Number 2 be?

8. Number 2 as a car, what could Number 5 be?

9. Number 7 as the sun, what could Number 2 be?

10. Number 1 as parents, what could Number 2 be?

11. Number 9 as cows, what could Number 4 be?

12. Number 2 as ice cream, what could number 3 be?

13. Number 6 as string, what could Number 2 be?

14. Number 5 as a tree, what could Number 9 be?

Comment...

Be flexible yourself when you evaluate the answers. For example, if a child thinks the "hair" in Question 4 looks something like a profile, why argue?

Suggested answers...

1. hammer; 2. ball; 3. icicle; 4. hair; 5. eyelashes; 6. anthill; 7. light bulb; 8. road; 9. moon; 10. child; 11. fence; 12. cone; 13. balloon; 14. leaves.

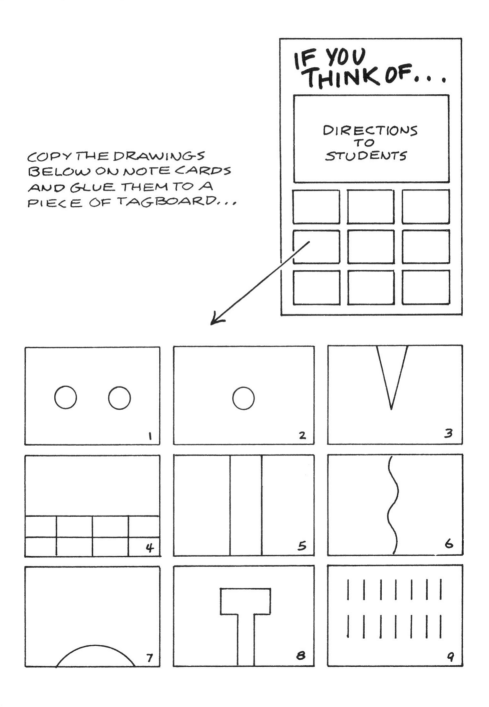

COPY THE DRAWINGS BELOW ON NOTE CARDS AND GLUE THEM TO A PIECE OF TAGBOARD...

IF YOU THINK OF...

DIRECTIONS TO STUDENTS

What You Use

About this center...

This activity is fun because it is much more open-ended than it appears at first glance. For example, the fact that the idea of sharpness (Number 1) can relate to objects as diverse as a knife and pencil should be interesting to children. A class discussion after they have finished with the center would probably be worthwhile, therefore. Stress that clothing, toy or food answers are not acceptable, and that no answer may be used twice. Why? Simply to make the assignment more challenging!

Materials needed...

Tagboard.

Directions to students...

Today, you will be thinking about things you use. You cannot use food, clothes, or toys as your answers, so you'll have to think hard! Do the work on your own paper.

Name one thing you use that...

1. needs to be sharp.
2. folds.
3. has numbers.
4. you use only once.
5. you can see through.
6. is straight.
7. you squeeze.
8. holds water.
9. has a handle.
10. makes a noise.
11. has a knob.
12. is white.
13. can be hung up.
14. is metal.
15. has buttons (or keys) you press.
16. is sticky.
17. you can tie.
18. you ride in.
19. will bend.
20. fits into something else.
21. has one or more holes.
22. has four legs.
23. fits in your pocket.
24. goes around.

Comment...

Some children may want the opportunity to list as many answers as they can for each category. If they do, fine. In fact, if you think your whole class is up to the challenge, change the directions and opt for quantity.

Suggested answers...

1. knife, pencil, scissors, crayon; 2. book, newspaper, napkin, blanket, pocket knife; 3. telephone, ruler, television set, radio, book; 4. napkin, bandage, toothpick, paper cup, staple; 5. magnifying glass, water glass, window, plastic wrap; 6. ruler, yardstick, pencil, crayon; 7. sponge, toothpaste tube; 8. glass, bathtub, sink, bucket; 9. toothbrush, broom, door, lunch box, car; 10. vacuum cleaner, mixer, television, radio, lawnmower; 11. door, television set, drawer, stove; 12. soap, napkin, bandage; paper, chalk, ceiling; 13. hanger, towel, toothbrush, telephone; 14. spoon, knife, fork, toaster; 15. telephone (some), computer, calculator, mixer; 16. tape, glue, paste, toothpaste; 17. thread, string, rope; 18. car, wagon, train, airplane; 19. rubber band, wire, hanger; 20. key, electric plug, light bulb, drawer; 21. toothbrush, key, bathtub, needle; 22. table, chair, bed; 23. coin, pocket knife, key, pencil; 24. egg beater, screwdriver, some clocks, can opener, fan.

YOU CAN MAKE THIS SIMPLE FIGURE WITH COLORED PAPER OR DRAW IT DIRECTLY ON A PIECE OF TAGBOARD.

WHAT YOU USE

DIRECTIONS TO STUDENTS

Rhyme Time

About this center...

When you think about it, the creation of a rhyming poem involves an interesting process that requires not only the feeling for rhythm and sound employed in finding the rhyme, but also the intellectual process involved in testing the rhyming word for plausibility in a particular context. In other words, it provides opportunity to practice creative, flexible thinking.

Materials needed...

Tagboard.

Directions to students...

Number your paper 1-20 and write the words you think should be used to finish these little poems.

1. I like butterflies,
   but not in pumpkin _____.

2. I'll pet a dog or pet a cat,
   but you can't make me _____ _____ _____.

3. If a lobster grabbed me by the toe,
   I'd ask it nicely to _____ _____.

4. The cat is running through the house.
   I think it must have _____ _____ _____.

5. If you eat all that cake,
   you will get a _____ _____.

6. A day that is hot and sunny
   will make your ice cream _____.

7. To eat a tulip or a daisy,
   you've got to be a little _____.

8. The octopus said, "Come here, please."
   "Let me give you a great big _____."

9. A lightning bug looks bright,
   only in the dark _____ _____.

10. "Watch out, or I will pop you soon,"
    said the pin to the _____.

11. I'd rather eat bugs
    than take _____ .

12. When a pelican makes a wish,
    it wishes for a lot _____ _____ .

13. If you were a hawk,
    you'd rather fly than _____ .

14. See that green thing on that log?
    I think it's probably a _____ .

15. There are double-o's in *book*.
    You'll also find two o's in _____ .

16. A hat on a giraffe
    would surely make you _____ .

17. Three plus four is seven.
    Seven plus four is _____ .

18. A smile is a frown
    turned upside _____ .

19. If a snail and a turtle ran a race,
    which do you think would win _____ _____ ?

20. See that giant in that tree?
    I hope he doesn't fall _____ _____ .

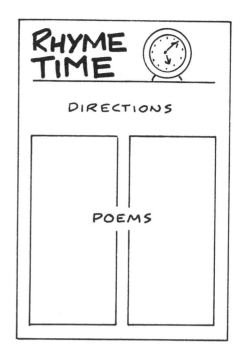

HAND LETTER TITLE. DRAW CLOCK. SEPARATE POEMS INTO TWO COLUMNS.

Comment...

Keep them true to the challenge. The answer "lazy" would not be acceptable for Number 7, even though it rhymes.

Suggested answers...

1. pies; 2. pet a rat (or bat); 3. let go; 4. seen a mouse; 5. tummy ache; 6. runny; 7. crazy; 8. squeeze; 9. at night; 10. balloon; 11. drugs; 12. of fish; 13. walk; 14. frog; 15. look (or cook, etc.); 16. laugh; 17. eleven; 18. down; 19. first place; 20. on me.

Shape Up!

About this center...

Here comes the structure again! This time, youngsters are instructed to examine the five shapes first and then to decide which shape is most appropriate for each drawing. The shapes are quite "neutral" for a reason — to make the challenge all the tougher. Flexible thinking is a must if students are to pull this one off successfully!

Materials needed...

Some note cards or a sheet of stiff paper for the shapes, an envelope, drawing paper, soft-leaded pencil. Tagboard for sign.

Directions to students...

Today, you are going to make five drawings. But wait a minute! There are some rules. Here they are:

Rule 1

You must draw these things:

> A robot   A bird   A monkey   A fish   A bug

Rule 2

You may use just one shape for each drawing — and you cannot use the shape more than once.

Rule 3

You must start your drawing by tracing all the way around the shape first.

Rule 4

You can finish your drawing in any way you like — with other shapes or lines — but we must still be able to see the shape you traced.

Good luck! The shapes are in the envelope. Look them over carefully before you begin so that you choose the best shape for each drawing. Put them back in the envelope after you finish.

Comment...

Although students must start with specific shapes, there is still plenty of room here for creative expression. Some good, hard thinking is also guaranteed, particularly for a youngster who tries to make a robot out of a shape which would probably be better for a bird or fish tail.

CUT AN INTERESTING
FREE-FORM SHAPE
TO CARRY OUT THE
THEME OF CENTER.

SHAPE UP!

DIRECTIONS
TO
STUDENTS

KEEP THE SHAPES IN AN
ENVELOPE AT THE CENTER.

CUT THE SHAPES SHOWN BELOW FROM STIFF PAPER.
MAKE THEM AT LEAST TWICE AS LARGE AS THESE...

BELOW - SOME POSSIBLE "SOLUTIONS."

About Our Room

About this center...

The subject of this center is a natural because it is part of every child's experience. If you wish, you could add some specific questions about your own room to this necessarily "generic" list.

Materials needed...

Tagboard.

Directions to students...

Here is your chance to do some thinking about where you are right now — in our classroom. Do the work on your own paper.

1. Look at the ceiling. Write down everything you notice.

2. Look at the place where the walls and the floor meet. What do you see?

3. Make a list of everything in our room that helps to keep things neat.

4. Is our blackboard really black? Why does it have to be a fairly dark color?

5. Why don't schoolrooms have mirrors?

6. Why don't schoolrooms have wallpaper?

7. How many things in our room run on electricity? Make a list.

8. What one thing in our room right now probably cost the school the most money to buy?

9. Why do schoolrooms have doors that close?

10. About how many times a day do you go through the door to the hall? (Count in and out as separate times.)

11. How many shoes are there in our room right now?

12. About how many pencils do you think there are in our room right now?

Comment...

The counting questions which are interspersed with the thinking questions are provided simply to change the pace and keep the interest. You could extend this activity by asking children to draw a "birds-eye" view of their room, or perhaps even of the whole school.

Suggested answers...

1. Answers will vary; 2. (There will be a molding of some kind); 3. Answers will vary; 4. so light-colored chalk marks will show; 5. They would be a distraction; 6. Paint costs less and you can keep painted walls clean more easily; 7. Answers will vary; 8. Answers will vary; 9. to keep things quiet so students can study; 10. Answers will vary; 11. Answers will vary; 12. Answers will vary.

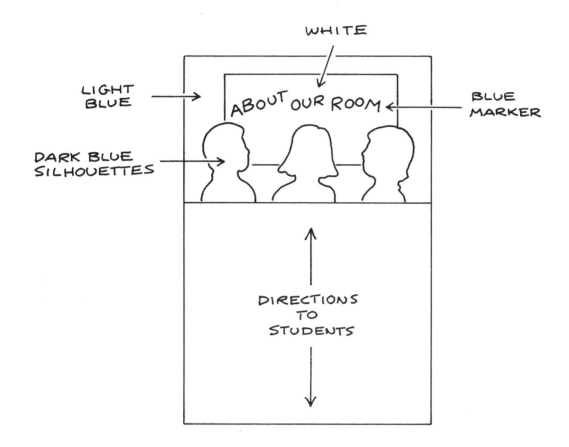

HERE IS AN EFFECTIVE PRESENTATION THAT IS VERY EASY TO MAKE. CUT THE SHAPES FROM COLORED PAPER AND GLUE TO TAGBOARD. START WITH A RECTANGLE OF LIGHT BLUE AND SUPERIMPOSE THE OTHER SHAPES.

Dip a Story

About this center...

First the fun, then the work! The easy part here is to use a spoon to dip a few random beans from a can. The work starts when students match the numbers written on the beans with the words on the chart and then attempt to weave all of those words into a little story. The element of chance, coupled with the hands-on nature of this activity, should motivate even your most reluctant writers.

Materials needed...

One soup can, 36 large lima beans, teaspoon. Tagboard for sign.

Directions to students...

Today, you are going to write a story, but you're going to start in a funny way. Here's how:

1. Use the spoon to dip three or four beans from the can (don't peek at the numbers.)

2. Match the numbers on your beans with the numbered words on the chart and write down those words.

3. Write the most interesting story you can using all of the words you have "dipped."

HERE IS THE WORD/NUMBER CHART. YOU COULD SAVE SOME TIME BY REPRODUCING THIS VERSION AND MOUNTING IT ON COLORED TAGBOARD . . .

tornado 1	tree 2	shark 3	house 4	elephant 5	window 6
girl 7	mud 8	teacher 9	boy 10	money 11	ring 12
eraser 13	milk 14	city 15	airplane 16	bug 17	pocket 18
gum 19	spider 20	monster 21	street 22	book 23	soap 24
park 25	dream 26	drum 27	recess 28	ditch 29	snow 30
pizza 31	ladder 32	test 33	gloves 34	worm 35	blanket 36

Comment...

You can make this assignment more difficult simply by asking children to dip into the can twice. If this center is really popular with your students — and we suspect it will be — you could make additional word charts of your own.

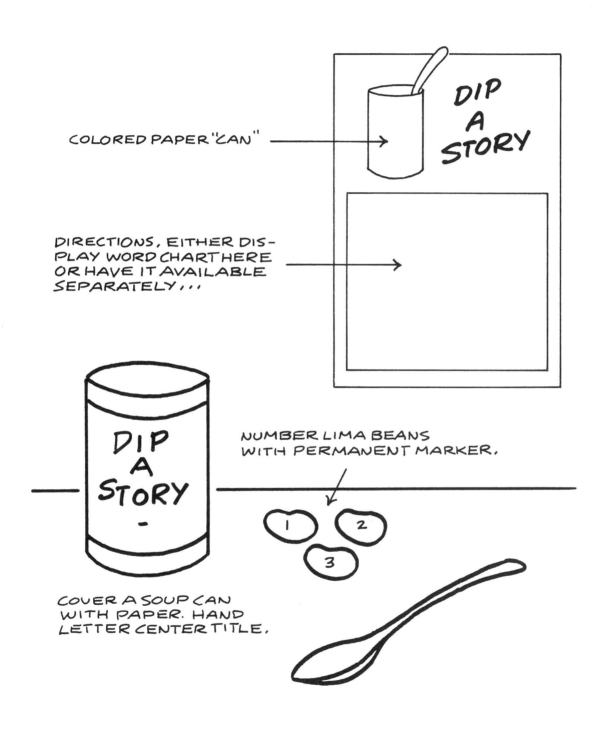

COLORED PAPER "CAN"

DIP A STORY

DIRECTIONS, EITHER DIS-
PLAY WORD CHART HERE
OR HAVE IT AVAILABLE
SEPARATELY...

DIP A STORY -

NUMBER LIMA BEANS
WITH PERMANENT MARKER.

1 2
3

COVER A SOUP CAN
WITH PAPER. HAND
LETTER CENTER TITLE.

Dots and Thoughts

About this center...

Students will take their cues from the placement of dots to determine which statement fits best with each dot picture. In preparing this center, be sure to make your dots more or less identical, so that you don't introduce any false clues. Advise children to read all of the statements first before writing their answers.

Materials needed...

Tagboard, nine note cards.

Directions to students...

Number your paper from 1-9 and then find one dot drawing that you think has something to do with each sentence. Be sure to look at all of the pictures and sentences first before you write your answers.

1. I lost a button.

2. I like hikes in the woods.

3. Let's go bowling!

4. Where did everybody go?

5. Here comes the parade.

6. The mosquitoes are bad tonight.

7. Listen when the teacher talks!

8. Pass the salt shaker.

9. We are playing hide-and-seek.

Suggested answers...

1. I
2. D
3. B
4. C
5. G
6. A
7. H
8. E
9. F

Comment...

This concept really involves some mental gymnastics, for in some cases the dots represent people (either in a seating pattern or in movement), while in other situations the dots stand for things as diverse as mosquitoes and holes in a salt shaker.

HAND LETTER WITH
COLORED MARKERS. $\longrightarrow$

DOTS
AND THOUGHTS

DIRECTIONS

TAGBOARD $\longrightarrow$

DRAWINGS

PUT THESE "DOT DRAWINGS" ON NOTE CARDS AND
GLUE TO TAGBOARD. MAKE THE DOTS FAIRLY LARGE.

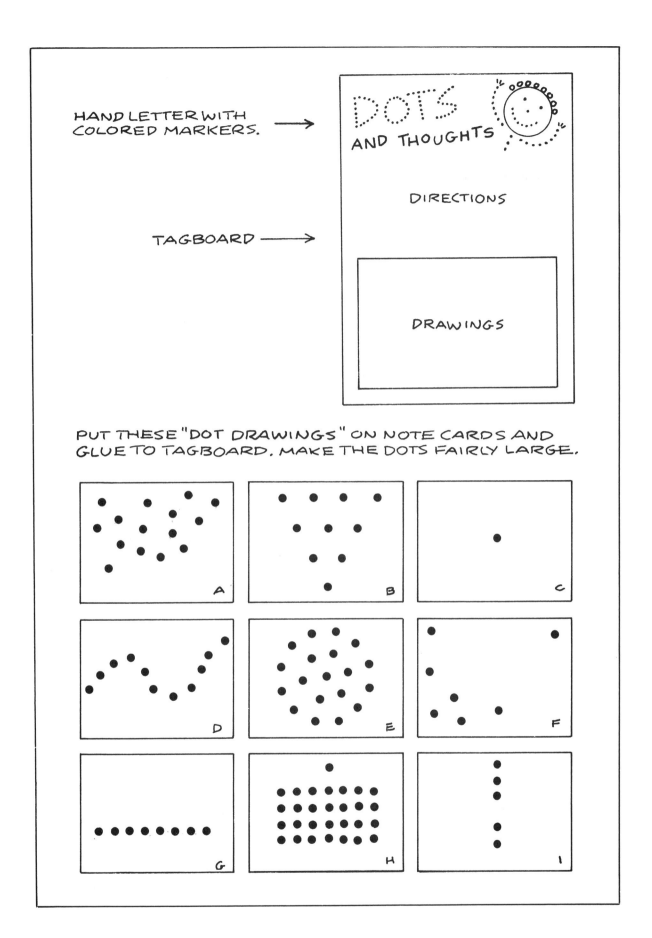

The Apple

About this center...

What we are after in this center is fluency of ideas. By using the apple as a constant, children are prompted to come from various directions to arrive at their answers.

Materials needed...

Tagboard.

Directions to students...

Think of an apple. Then write your answers on your own paper.

1. Name three things that are heavier than an apple.

2. Name three things that are lighter than an apple.

3. Name three things that are rounder than an apple.

4. Name three things that are sweeter than an apple.

5. Name three things that are harder than an apple.

6. Name three things that are smaller than an apple.

7. Name three things that have thicker skin than an apple.

8. Name three things you could balance on top of an apple.

9. Name three things that are as red as an apple.

10. Name three things that would break if you dropped an apple on them.

11. Name three things you could hide under an apple.

12. Name one thing that could *eat* an apple.

Comment...

The centerpiece of this challenge is the apple, but don't have a real apple available at the center. The point is for students to handle solutions to this activity in their heads!

Suggested answers...

1. car, dictionary, sofa; 2. safety pin, envelope, bug; 3. ball, globe, orange; 4. cookies, candy, cake; 5. pencil, book, plate; 6. button, grape, peanut; 7. lemon, watermelon, tangerine; 8. thimble, box, ruler; 9. ketchup, fire truck, stop sign; 10. egg, cracker, cookie; 11. stamp, paper clip, raisin; 12. me.

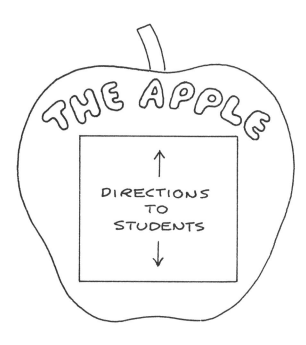

CUT APPLE SHAPE FROM RED TAGBOARD.
ADD "PLUMP" LETTERS CUT FROM A
CONTRASTING COLOR – LIGHT GREEN
OR LIGHT BLUE WOULD BE EFFECTIVE...

A Look at a Book

About this center...

Books are to read, aren't they? Yes, but a book is also a remarkable mechanical invention. One interesting aspect of this activity involves the use of a book as an "object" to be investigated. There are also some entertaining word hunts and conceptual challenges.

Materials needed...

A hardcover book about an inch thick, ruler. Tagboard for sign.

Directions to students...

You will need to use the book to answer these questions. Do the work on your own paper.

1. Why is the cover of the book thicker — and a little larger — than the pages?

2. What do you think has been done to keep the pages from falling out?

3. Turn to page 18. Find (and write on your own paper) a one-letter word, a two-letter word, and a three-letter word. Can you also find words on this page which have four, five, six, and seven letters? Make the longest list you can without skipping any numbers.

4. The long skinny part of a book's cover is called the spine. Why is the title of a book usually printed on the spine?

5. Use the ruler to measure the thickness of the book. Then find the number of pages in the book. About how many pages would it take to make a book two inches thick?

6. Stand the book up with the cover spread out slightly (so that it looks like a tent) and make a list of five living things that could crawl through the opening without touching any of the pages.

7. Why is learning something from a book sometimes better than learning it from television?

8. Why is learning something from television sometimes better than learning it from a book?

9. Find the first word on pages 7, 14, and 24. Write them down and then try to write a sentence using all three words. (You may use other words, too.)

10. Find the third word on page 9, the last word on page 62, and the tenth word on page 14. Write another sentence using those words.

Comment...

You may want to examine the book you're using before you write the instructions for the last two activities. If the words in Number 9 or 10 turn out to be "an, the, on," change the page number.

Suggested answers...

1. to protect the pages; 2. They have been glued and sewn; 3. Answers will vary; 4. so you will know what book it is when it is on a shelf; 5. Answers will vary; 6. Answers will vary; 7. because there can be more detail and you can go back to it many times; 8. You can actually see and hear what is happening; 9. Answers will vary; 10. Answers will vary.

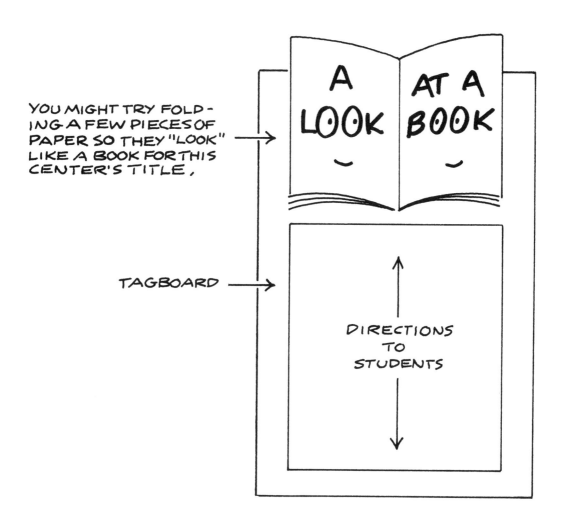

YOU MIGHT TRY FOLD-ING A FEW PIECES OF PAPER SO THEY "LOOK" LIKE A BOOK FOR THIS CENTER'S TITLE,

A LOOK AT A BOOK

TAGBOARD

DIRECTIONS TO STUDENTS

Out of Place

About this center...

In this activity, the student will be looking at the checked item and deciding why it doesn't belong. Notice that in several lists, the words are the same. Just the check mark changes.

Materials needed...

Tagboard.

Directions to students...

In each of these sets of words, one word doesn't belong. It is the word with the check mark beside it. Your job is to tell why it doesn't belong. Do the work on your own paper, and be sure to look at the example before you start.

Example: Rice
Cheese
Eggs
✔ Scissors
Beans

Your answer is: "not food"

Here we go!

1. Paper Clip
   Nail
   ✔ Paper
   Toaster
   Penny

2. Swiss Cheese
   Notebook Paper
   Tennis Shoe
   Doughnut
   ✔ Postcard

3. Paper Clip
   Hat
   Toaster
   Penny
   ✔ Leaf

4. Lettuce
   ✔ Marshmallow
   Peas
   Grass
   Celery

5. Lettuce
   Marshmallow
   Peas
   ✔ Grass
   Celery

6. Robin
   Duck
   Parrot
   ✔ Lizard
   Goose

7. Sun
   Toaster
   Oven
   Iron
   ✔ Mixer

8. ✔ Sun
   Toaster
   Oven
   Iron
   Mixer

9. Policeman
   Nurse
   Soldier
   Airline Pilot
   ✔ Teacher

10. Period
    Comma
    ✔ Sentence
    Hyphen
    Question Mark

11. Itch
    Scratch
    Wave
    ✔ See
    Rub

12. Box
    Envelope
    ✔ Stamp
    Folder
    Can

13. Box
    Envelope
    Stamp
    Folder
    ✔ Can

14. Smile
    Frown
    Wink
    ✔ Tears
    Grin

15. Nose
    Eyes
    Ears
    ✔ Legs
    Eyebrows

16. ✔ Nose
    Eyes
    Ears
    Legs
    Eyebrows

Comment...

Emphasis here is on the "why," and that will take some analytical thinking about the "what" as children think about the characteristics of each item. You could make this a bit more rigorous by requiring that answers be given in the form of complete sentences.

Suggested answers...

1. not metal; 2. no holes; 3. not man-made; 4. not green; 5. not food we eat; 6. not a bird; 7. not something which produces heat; 8. not something found in a house (also not man-made); 9. not a job which requires a uniform; 10. not a punctuation mark; 11. not something done with the hands; 12. not something which holds something (container); 13. not made out of paper; 14. not a facial expression; 15. not found on the face; 16. not something that comes in pairs.

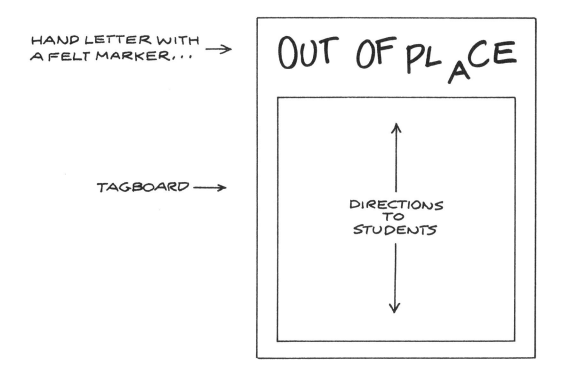

Shipwrecked!

About this center...

Here is a classic stranded-on-a-desert-island scenario. Youngsters will have to make some important choices in order to survive. They will also have to give reasons for their choices, a requirement which will keep the activity on a serious level.

Materials needed...

Tagboard.

Directions to students...

Hurry! Your ship is sinking and there will only be time to save one thing from each of the 20 pairs below. That's the bad news. The good news is that there is an island nearby. (But nobody lives on the island and you'll probably be stuck there all alone for a long time.) Number your paper 1-20. Tell which thing you would save and give a short reason why.

1. Shoes — Socks
2. Calendar — Clock
3. Shovel — Rake
4. Mirror — Compass
5. Cup — Pan
6. Ball — Yo-yo
7. Coat — Blanket
8. Gloves — Hat
9. Toothbrush — Comb
10. Scissors — Pocket Knife

11. Soap — Toothpaste
12. Fork — Spoon
13. Screwdriver — Hammer
14. Rope — Chain
15. Envelope — Stamp
16. Dictionary — Encyclopedia
17. Raincoat — Umbrella
18. Fishhook — Fishing Pole
19. Matches — Flashlight
20. Crayon — Pencil

Comment...

You might wish to have a group discussion and even take a vote on the 20 choices. You're sure to get some spirited arguments as your Robinson Crusoes compare ideas.

Suggested answers...

1. shoes (they provide better protection); 2. calendar (days are more important than hours to castaways); 3. shovel (it can do more things); 4. mirror (for signaling); 5. pan (could be used for cooking and drinking); 6. yo-yo (one person can play with it); 7. blanket (could be used for shade, cape or cover at night); 8. gloves (you could probably make a hat, but not gloves); 9. toothbrush (clean teeth more important than neat hair); 10. pocket knife (it can do more things); 11. soap (you could probably brush your teeth with soap but couldn't get clean with toothpaste); 12. spoon (more uses); 13. hammer (more uses); 14. rope (more uses); 15. envelope (could use the paper); 16. encyclopedia (would probably have more information useful for survival); 17. raincoat (more uses, including warmth); 18. fishhook (a fishhook would be much harder to make); 19. matches (fire more important); 20. pencil (better for writing and would last longer).

USE A COLORED FELT MARKER TO MAKE THIS SIMPLE DRAWING. DO THE LETTERING BY HAND WITH A MARKER OF ANOTHER COLOR.

TAGBOARD———>

SHIPWRECKED!

DIRECTIONS TO STUDENTS

Make a Box!

About this center...

There are times you should ask a student to do something which may elicit the response, "I can't." Your answer should be, "Yes, you can." If this box project teaches students nothing else, it will teach them to make the best of a tough situation. Get set for some ungainly boxes, and tell your students you can't make a perfect one either. *Note:* The boxes should not have lids. The projects in Step 2 would not work well if they did.

Materials needed......

Plenty of cellophane tape, scissors, ruler, pencil, construction paper. Tagboard for sign.

Directions to students...

Step 1

Your first job is to make a box. You can make it in any way you like, but you can use just one piece of paper. You can use the tape, scissors, ruler, and pencil however you wish. After you have made your box, go on to Step 2.

Step 2

Now that you have a box, find some way to turn it into one of the things listed below. You can use other paper and marker pens if you wish.

A house

A wagon with someone riding in it

A basket with food in it

A car or truck

Comment......

Many children will tackle this problem by cutting out a bottom and then putting the sides on one at a time. Let them! After the project is completed, it might be interesting to bring a couple of commercial boxes to class and take them apart to see how they were made (or you can show them how to make the boxes that have been drawn here).

MAKE A FREEHAND DRAWING OF A BOX FOR THIS CENTER. DON'T PROVIDE AN ACTUAL BOX FOR CHILDREN TO SEE.

TAGBOARD ———————→

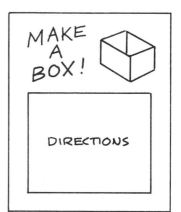

MAKE A BOX!

DIRECTIONS

THERE ARE LOTS OF WAYS TO HANDLE THE SECOND PART OF THIS CENTER. HERE ARE A FEW IDEAS.

HOUSE

WAGON

BASKET

CAR

HERE ARE A COUPLE OF SIMPLE BOXES YOU CAN MAKE . . .

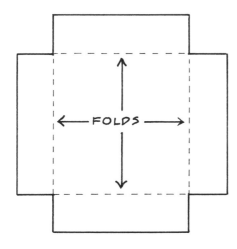

FOLDS

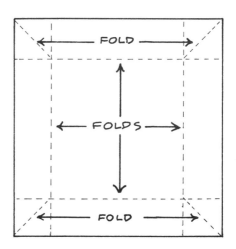

FOLD

FOLDS

FOLD

What Does a Dog Know?

About this center...

Although not every child will have a dog, it is the assumption that they all will have had at least some experience with dogs. Even if a few children have had very limited contact, this is probably within their capabilities.

Materials needed...

Tagboard.

Directions to students...

How smart is a dog? Let's think about it. Answer these dog questions on your own paper.

1. Below is a list of 20 words. A smart dog might know 10 of them, but it almost surely would not know the other 10. List the 10 words you think a dog might know.

No	Sit
Sure	Noun
Money	Down
Food	Dream
Taste	Bad
Car	Stick
Dog	Honest
Good	Ball
Any	Triangle
Small	Above

2. Pick one of the words you think a dog might not know and tell why a dog probably wouldn't know it.

3. List three things (not words) a dog might know.

4. Do you think a dog would recognize a photograph of its owner? Why or why not?

5. Dogs bark at cats, but they don't bark at bugs. Why?

Comment...

About Number 1: Children may not provide all of the same answers we have, but they should grasp the idea that dogs can be trained to respond to conventional commands. Also, they should at least intuit the idea that a dog would have a hard time with an abstract concept, such as a triangle. (Of course, you could train a dog to expect food every time you said, "triangle," but that's another story. No need to bring Pavlov into this...)

Suggested answers...

1. no, food, car, dog, good, sit, down, bad, stick, ball; 2. Answers will vary; 3. location of its house, where it is fed, family members, other pets, how to ask to go outside, where it buried a bone, etc.; 4. No, dogs aren't smart enough to understand that a photograph "stands for" a person; 5. Cats are more their size and do things that make dogs mad, such as eating their food; bugs are small and, with the exception of fleas and ticks, are not much bother.

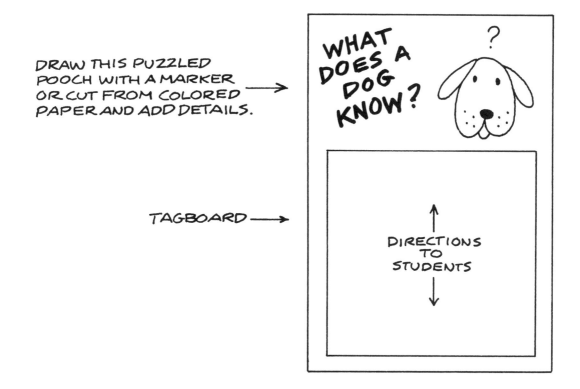

Trix with Pix

About this center...

Why toothpicks? Simply because a picture made in this way offers a surprise. You'll notice that each toothpick picture is made with just five segments. This helps to give the pictures some simplicity and a uniform look. Cut (or break) the toothpicks into the proper length and then glue them securely to squares of colored tagboard. It will take a little patience, but you can use the center over and over.

Materials needed...

Tagboard, toothpicks, white glue.

Directions to students...

Here are 12 toothpick pictures. Match the number of the picture with the 12 words. Do the work on your own paper.

Face	Icicle
Fence	Teeter-totter
Hanger	Flower
Giant	Juggler
Family	Fish
Bed	Flag

BONUS: Besides being made out of toothpicks, what do all 12 pictures have in common?

Comment...

Children should have a great deal of fun with this project. They'll have to work at it, however, because the abstractions are not always as easy as they appear.

Suggested answers...

1. family; 2. hanger; 3. bed; 4. flag; 5. icicle; 6. fish; 7. fence; 8. giant; 9. juggler; 10. teeter-totter; 11. face; 12. flower. BONUS: All pictures use five toothpick parts.

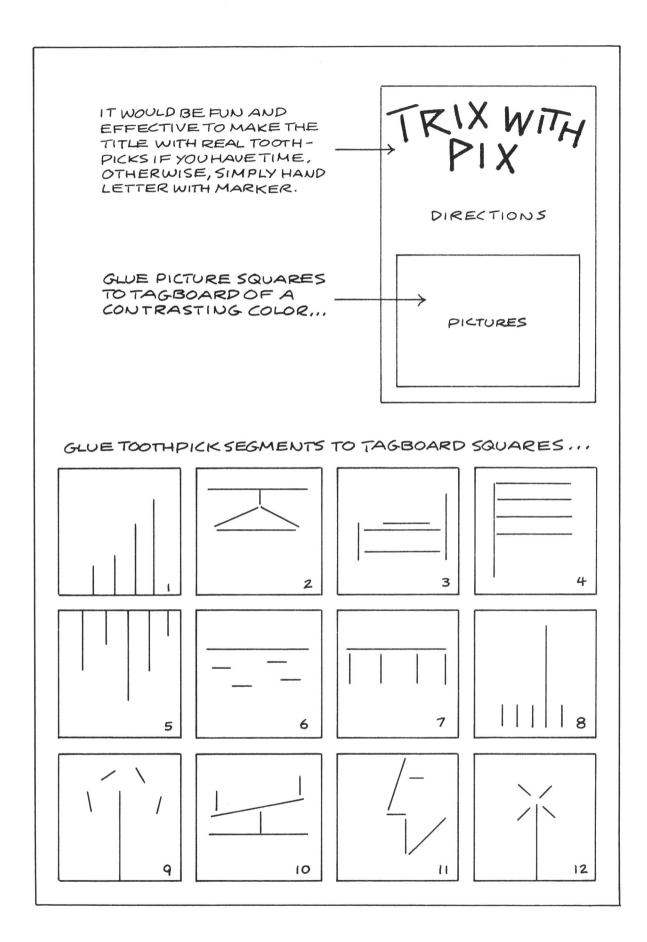

IT WOULD BE FUN AND EFFECTIVE TO MAKE THE TITLE WITH REAL TOOTH-PICKS IF YOU HAVE TIME, OTHERWISE, SIMPLY HAND LETTER WITH MARKER.

TRIX WITH PIX

DIRECTIONS

GLUE PICTURE SQUARES TO TAGBOARD OF A CONTRASTING COLOR...

PICTURES

GLUE TOOTHPICK SEGMENTS TO TAGBOARD SQUARES...

1   2   3   4

5   6   7   8

9   10   11   12

Thinking Things

About this center...

Don't shy away from using this center because you have to make the four shapes. They can be made in five minutes. The manipulation involved in this activity is sure to be welcomed by your "hands-on" enthusiasts.

Materials needed...

Note card (for you to use in making the shapes), chalkboard eraser, cellophane tape. Tagboard for sign.

Directions to students...

Use the four paper shapes to help you answer the following questions. Answer with the number you see on the shape.

1. Which two objects have the most to do with a house?

2. Think of Object 4 as something you find in some houses. What could it be?

3. Can you think of anything in a schoolroom that is something like Object 3? What is it?

4. Which of the objects has the most to do with a car?

5. Name one important way in which Objects 3 and 4 are alike.

6. Put Object 3 on the table so that it looks like a tent. Which other object is easiest to balance on top of Object 3?

7. Roll Object 1 across the table.
   a. What does the tape have to do with how it rolls?
   b. Where is the tape each time the object stops?

8. Each of the four objects is strong enough to hold the eraser up off the desk. Write a sentence about how you can do it.

9. How many folds are there in all the objects put together?

10. Try stacking all of the objects on top of each other. How did you do it? Answer by giving the number on the bottom object, next to the bottom, and on up to the top.

Comment...

The idea that the same object (Number 3) can be used to represent a roof (Question 1), a book (Question 3), and a tent (Question 6) leaves no question that flexible thinking is involved in this project.

Suggested answers...

1. Objects 2 and 3 (walls and roof); 2. stairs; 3. book; 4. Object 1 (wheel); 5. They form triangles and have folds; 6. Object 4; 7. a. The tape keeps it from rolling smoothly, b. on the bottom; 8. I put the objects on their edges; 9. 12; 10. The easiest way is (from bottom to top): 1, 3, 2, 4, but there can be other solutions.

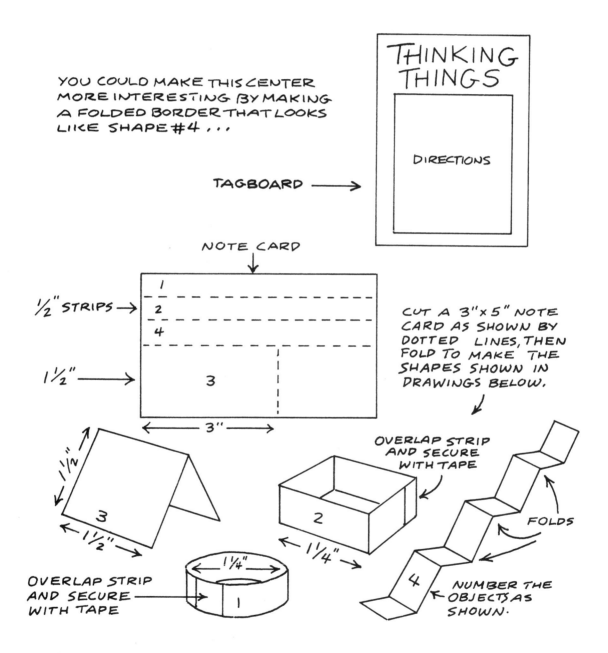

YOU COULD MAKE THIS CENTER MORE INTERESTING BY MAKING A FOLDED BORDER THAT LOOKS LIKE SHAPE #4 . . .

THINKING THINGS

DIRECTIONS

TAGBOARD ——→

NOTE CARD

½" STRIPS →

1½" ——→

3"

CUT A 3" x 5" NOTE CARD AS SHOWN BY DOTTED LINES, THEN FOLD TO MAKE THE SHAPES SHOWN IN DRAWINGS BELOW.

1½"

3

1½"

OVERLAP STRIP AND SECURE WITH TAPE

OVERLAP STRIP AND SECURE WITH TAPE

1¼"

1

2

1¼"

FOLDS

4

NUMBER THE OBJECTS AS SHOWN.

Thinking Links

About this center...

The objective here is to foster fluency of thought. Students will be going from one concept to another in rapid succession in response to connecting clues. Emphasize that the same answer cannot be used more than once.

Materials needed...

Tagboard.

Directions to students...

Put on your thinking cap for this one! Write the answers on your own paper, and don't use the same answer more than once. Good luck!

1. Think of the color of a cloud. (Write the color on your paper.)

2. Think of something that color which is soft.

3. Think of something soft that is smaller than your hand.

4. Think of something smaller than your hand which has holes.

5. Think of something which has holes that you can eat.

6. Think of something you can eat which is round.

7. Think of something which is round that you can slice.

8. Think of something you can slice that is juicy.

9. Think of something juicy that is red.

10. Think of something red that you see by a street.

11. Think of something you see by a street which is made of wood.

12. Think of something made of wood which you find in a house.

13. Think of something you find in a house which is flat.

14. Think of something flat which your feet can touch.

15. Think of something your feet can touch which is cold.

16. Think of something which is cold that is...whew!...the COLOR OF A CLOUD.

Comment...

After all the children have gone through these challenges, share the results with the class. It should be interesting to note the diversity of answers in some cases and the similarity in others. There might even be graphing possibilities.

Suggested answers...

1. white, pink, grey; 2. bubble gum, gum, cotton ball; 3. eraser, marshmallow; 4. button, salt or pepper shaker, needle; 5. cracker, Swiss cheese; 6. pizza, cookie; 7. grapefruit, apple; 8. tomato, orange; 9. watermelon, strawberry; 10. stop sign, stop light, fire hydrant (some); 11. telephone pole, fence; 12. door, pencil, furniture; 13. floor, table, ceiling; 14. carpet, sidewalk; 15. snow, water, tile; 16. milk (if cloud is white); lemonade or soda pop (if cloud is pink).

USE A PAPER CHAIN BORDER TO CARRY OUT THE THEME OF THIS CENTER... →

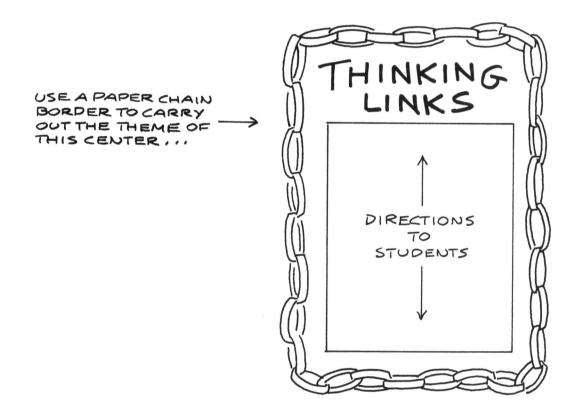

THINKING LINKS

DIRECTIONS TO STUDENTS

Mystery Marks

About this center...

Be prepared for some long, awkward sentences as children describe each of the drawings in detail. The point here is not sentence structure, but close observation and communication concerning what is seen.

Materials needed...

Tagboard, nine note cards.

Directions to the student...

Look carefully at the drawings on the nine cards. Then write one long, long sentence which describes everything exactly as you see it on each card.

 Example: "I see a large circle with a small circle in the middle, and the large circle touches the bottom and top of the rectangle."

Start each of your sentences with "I see." Number your sentences 1-9 so we can tell which picture you are describing.

Comment...

You may find that nine descriptions entail too much writing in certain situations. If that is the case, simply have students choose three or four drawings to describe. Another thought: What if a student describes Number 8 by saying, "I see four witches' hats with three space ships coming toward them."? Well, you should probably commend the student for the imaginative approach, but gently insist upon a more objective description.

Suggested answers...

1. I see a small rectangle inside a big rectangle and there is a dot in the middle of the small rectangle.

2. I see an X that touches each corner of the card and there is a dot in the middle of the X.

3. I see nine dashes in the middle of the card that seem to form a circle.

4. I see two lines in the middle of the card that are straight up and down and one of the lines is longer than the other and there is a dot above each of the lines.

5. I see a circle in each corner of the card and there is a triangle in the middle.

6. I see a long, wiggly line in the middle of the card and the line is not closed and there is an X in the middle of the shape made by the line.

7. I see five curved lines in five spaces that are made by four straight lines.

8. I see four triangles of the same size at the bottom of the card and there are three circles above the spaces between the triangles.

9. I see three wiggly lines coming down from the top of the card and there is a straight line across all of the wiggly lines.

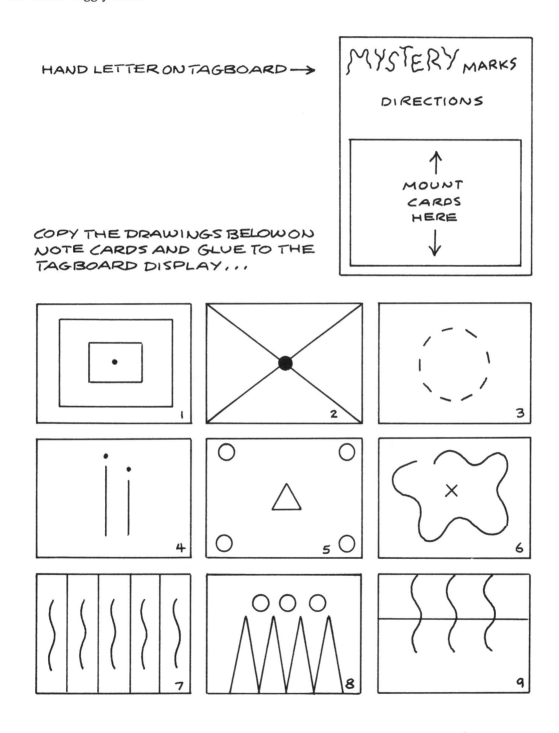

41

Big Ideas about Little Things

About this center...

An egg carton becomes the display case for a dozen common objects — and some interesting thinking should ensue. For the most part, youngsters will be asked to observe, rather than manipulate, the objects, and be sure to stress that nibbling is against the rules. Once you have the center prepared, there should be very little upkeep as various children work through the challenges.

Materials needed...

The bottom half of one egg carton, and the following objects: raisin, paper clip, wad of paper, button, small rock, piece of popped popcorn, popcorn kernel, uncancelled stamp with a value of 5¢ or more, screw-on bottle cap from a soft drink container, small piece of chalk, penny, and one unshelled peanut. The various compartments in the egg carton should be lettered with a permanent marker. Tagboard for sign.

Directions to students...

Look at the objects in the egg carton. Then, on your own paper, answer the questions by writing the correct letter (or letters) for each answer. (Each object has its own letter.)

Example: If the question were: "Which objects are metal?" your answer would be, "B, I and K."

Hint: Think very carefully, because often you will have several letters for an answer.

1. Which of these things has the most value?

2. Which are not man-made?

3. Which two things did (*teacher's name*) change the most from their original shape?

4. Which five things are made to be used with something else?

5. Which of these things could you write with?

6. Which of these things have something to do with paper?

7. Which of these things have some straight lines?

8. Which of these things looks most like a cloud?

9. Which two things have the most wrinkles?

42

10. Which of these things is the oldest?

11. Which of these things would burn?

12. If you dropped all of these things from a tall building, which one would probably break into the most pieces?

13. Which of these things have a different front and back?

14. Which of these things might come in a different color?

15. Which of these things have something separate inside?

Comment...

Careful! The suggested answers are subject to interpretation. If it is a stormy day outside, a child might give "raisin," rather than "popcorn" as the answer to Number 8.

Suggested answers...

1. H.
2. A, E, F, G, L.
3. C, F.
4. B, D, H, I, J.
5. J, maybe E.
6. B, C, H.
7. B, C, H, J.
8. F.
9. A, C.
10. E.
11. A, C, F, G, H, L, maybe D (if not metal).
12. J.
13. D, H, I, K.
14. Everything but F, G, K, L.
15. L.

TAGBOARD ⟶

BIG IDEAS
- ABOUT -
LITTLE THINGS

↑
DIRECTIONS
TO
STUDENTS
↓

RIGHT -
A DIAGRAM OF
EGG CARTON.
USE PERMA-
NENT MARKER
FOR LETTERS.

A	B	C	D	E	F
RAISIN	PAPER CLIP	WAD OF PAPER	BUTTON	ROCK	POPCORN (POPPED)
G	H	I	J	K	L
POPCORN KERNEL	5¢ STAMP	BOTTLE CAP	SMALL PIECE OF CHALK	PENNY	PEANUT IN SHELL

2½ Circles

About this center...

The impetus for this center goes back to an idea we have expressed often in our materials... that the best creative thinking does not take place in a free-for-all situation but rather in a setting where there is some structure. In this case, the three shapes provide both the limitations and the "possibilities."

Materials needed...

One envelope, stiff paper (for the drawing templates), 8½" × 11" paper. Tagboard for sign.

Directions to students...

To do this center, you must be able to follow directions and use your imagination.

Directions:

1. Begin by folding the piece of paper in half and then in half again to divide it into four rectangles. Number the rectangles 1-4. (Put the numbers in the lower right-hand corner of each rectangle.) Then turn the paper over and number the rectangles on the back 5-6-7-8.

2. Next, your job is to make eight little drawings of the eight things listed below. But... each drawing must include ALL three shapes. The shapes can touch each other or be partway on top of each other if you wish, but you can't use the shapes more than one time for each drawing. (You may add any other lines you need.)

3. Here are the things you are to draw:

   1. A baby buggy   5. An owl

   2. A happy clown   6. A funny car

   3. A sad clown   7. An octopus

   4. A monster   8. A strange fish

Hint: You may want to use an extra piece of paper to make some little idea drawings before you draw in the rectangles.

Comment...

It is probably a good idea to encourage the children to make a lot of little idea sketches before executing their finished work. Also, don't display any of the drawings before everyone has had time at the center. Children are natural copycats.

USE TAGBOARD OF A
CONTRASTING COLOR →
FOR THE "MOUSE."

2½
CIRCLES

TAGBOARD →

↑
DIRECTIONS
TO
STUDENTS
↓

CUT THESE SHAPES
FROM STIFF PAPER,
KEEP THEM IN AN
ENVELOPE AT THE
CENTER . . .

←— 2¼" —→

←3/4"→   ←3/4"→

HERE ARE SOME TYPICAL "SOLUTIONS" TO THE DRAWING
PROBLEMS. OF COURSE THERE ARE MANY POSSIBILITIES.

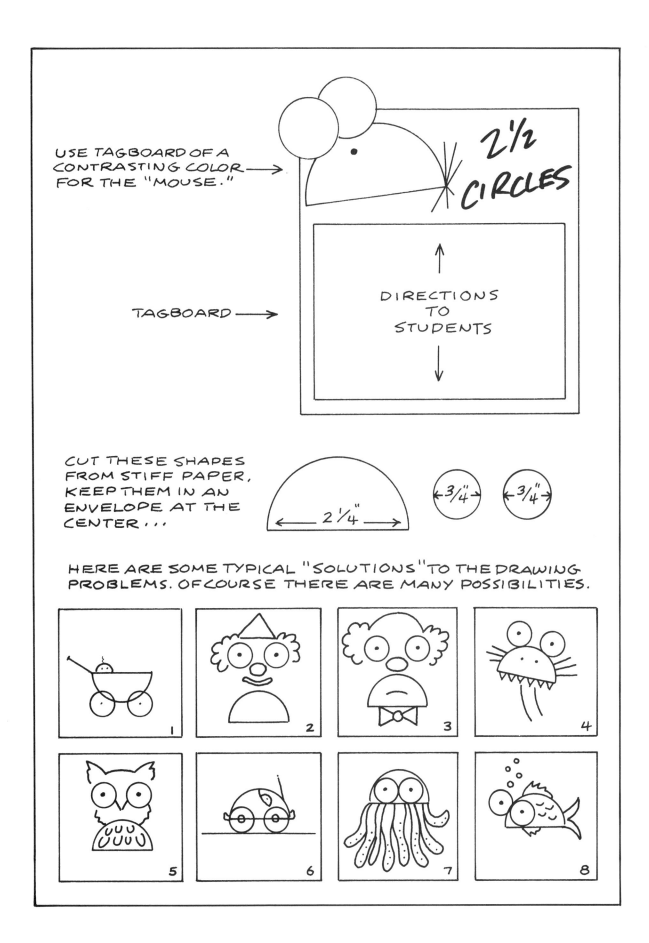

Words about Circles

About this center...

Although the initial challenge involves observation, the real challenge in this center becomes one of communication — of finding a good way to relate what is seen.

Materials needed...

Tagboard.

Directions to students...

What is happening to the circles? Try to write at least three different things you can say for sure about each picture. (Write more if you can.) See example for Number 1.

Example:
1. There are eight circles. The circles are all touching. There are two bigger circles. The circles are all in a row.

Comment...

This activity may not have children jumping up and down with enthusiasm, but it encourages disciplined thought and expression. Just think of the trouble many adults have in giving street directions.

Regarding the suggested answers, keep in mind that there are other valid statements that can be made in every case.

Suggested answers...

2. There are four circles. The smallest circle is in the middle. The circles are all different sizes. There is a straight line touching the biggest circle.

3. There is a straight line. One circle is touching the line. Another circle of the same size touches the circle that is touching the straight line.

4. Eight little circles touch a big circle. The eight little circles are the same size. The eight little circles each have a dot in them.

5. There are five circles. The three largest circles do not touch each other. The two smaller circles touch each other and are the same size.

6. Two circles are in a rectangle. There is a big circle and a small circle. Both circles are touching the edge of the rectangle.

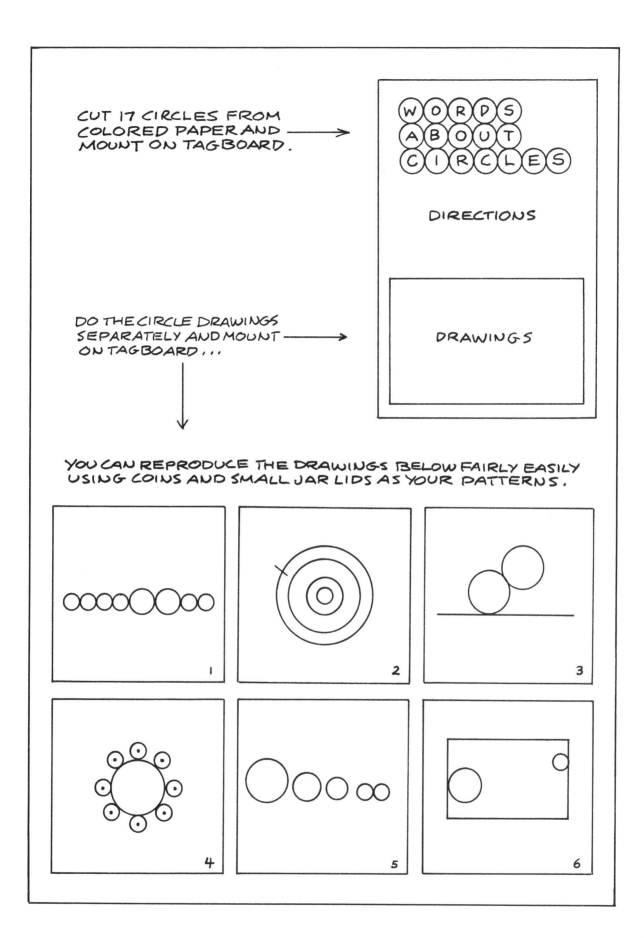

CUT 17 CIRCLES FROM
COLORED PAPER AND
MOUNT ON TAGBOARD.

WORDS
ABOUT
CIRCLES

DIRECTIONS

DO THE CIRCLE DRAWINGS
SEPARATELY AND MOUNT
ON TAGBOARD...

DRAWINGS

YOU CAN REPRODUCE THE DRAWINGS BELOW FAIRLY EASILY
USING COINS AND SMALL JAR LIDS AS YOUR PATTERNS.

1

2

3

4

5

6

A Date with a Plate

About this center...

Since a paper plate is concave rather than flat, it will be somewhat difficult for children to work with. That difficulty is the real point of this center, for the process of making uncooperative material "behave" requires thought, patience and imagination. The two subjects — elephant and fish — have been chosen because they have characteristics (trunk, fins or tail) that have something to do with the fluted edge of the plate. An astute child should notice this and will probably try to take advantage of it.

Materials needed....

Inexpensive paper plates with fluted edges (two for each child), cellophane or masking tape, felt markers. Tagboard and extra plate for sign.

Directions to students...

Your job today: Using just one paper plate for each thing, make...

1. an elephant's head.

2. a fish.

Here are some rules.

- Use one plate for each thing you make.

- You must cut the plate apart in some way and put the pieces together with the tape.

- You must use at least three pieces of the plate for each thing you make.

- You must use most of the plate.

- You cannot just make a drawing on the plate and cut it out.

- You can use the markers in any way you wish — but only after you have finished cutting and taping.

— Good luck!

Comment...

Remember, what we're after here is not art with a capital A, but thinking with a capital T. When everyone has finished, display the work fearlessly. Your displays will be light years ahead of those boring hand turkeys!

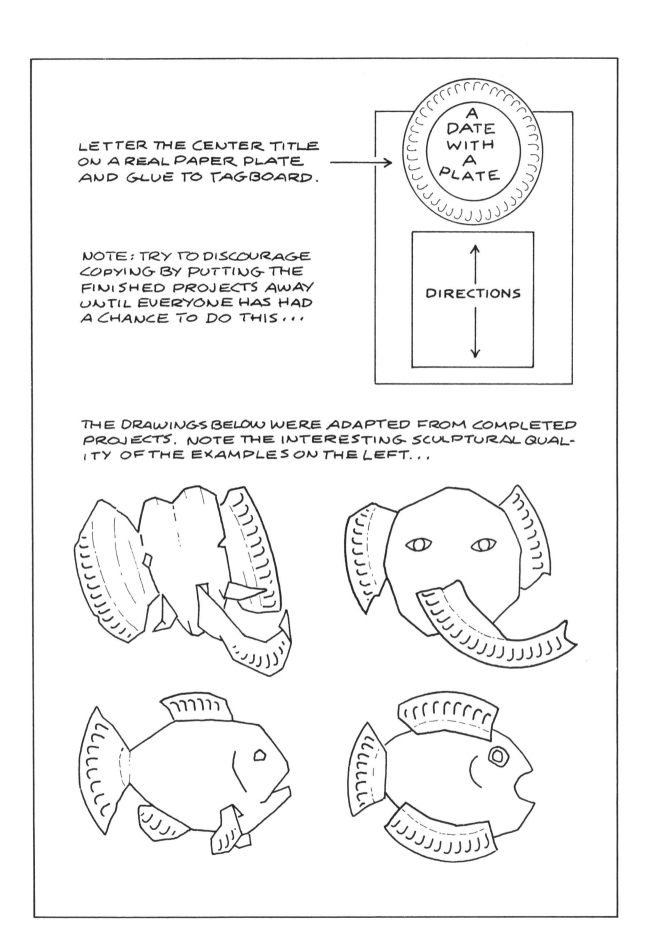

LETTER THE CENTER TITLE ON A REAL PAPER PLATE AND GLUE TO TAGBOARD.

A DATE WITH A PLATE

DIRECTIONS

NOTE: TRY TO DISCOURAGE COPYING BY PUTTING THE FINISHED PROJECTS AWAY UNTIL EVERYONE HAS HAD A CHANCE TO DO THIS...

THE DRAWINGS BELOW WERE ADAPTED FROM COMPLETED PROJECTS. NOTE THE INTERESTING SCULPTURAL QUALITY OF THE EXAMPLES ON THE LEFT...

Down the Middle

About this center...

This center involves a simple concept, but it is sure to encourage some thoughtful writing. We have attempted to provide words which are either interesting in themselves (giant, spotted) or are difficult to work into a sentence without using them as the first or last word (how, slowly).

Materials needed...

Tagboard.

TRY PRESENTING THIS ACTIVITY ON A LONG, SKINNY FORMAT FOR INTEREST. USE ONE COLOR FOR THE ARROW AND ANOTHER FOR THE VERTICAL PART.

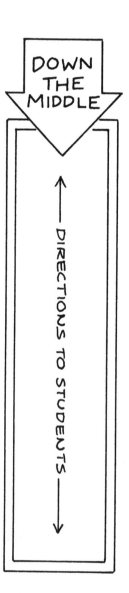

DOWN THE MIDDLE

DIRECTIONS TO STUDENTS

Directions to students...

Write the words down the middle of your own paper. Then build a sentence around each word on the list. Make your sentences as interesting as you can. One rule: None of the words below can be used as the first or last words in your sentences.

For example, you could use the first word on the list this way:
An angry *dinosaur* shakes the ground.

Here are the words — down the middle!

dinosaur

bedtime

run

dust

awful

care

bug

up

giant

slowly

hungry

how

cold

spotted

ship

everyone

Comment...

A way to make the project more difficult for sophisticated students would be to specify that the articles, a, an, the, cannot be used at the beginning of a sentence.

Another possibility would be to offer two seemingly unconnected words for students to build into the middle of a fanciful sentence. For example: dinosaur — blue. "When a dinosaur gets angry, its tongue turns blue and its eyes start to glow."

If this interests you, here is a list of "doubles": bedtime — turtle; run — hands; dust — water; awful — umbrella; care — giggle; bug — purse; up — singing; giant — tiny; slowly — flat; hungry — library; how — tooth; cold — purple; spotted — elbow; ship — three; everyone — wrinkles.

Your Face

About this center...

What's more compelling than a face — especially when it is your own? In this activity, students are encouraged to think about something they see everyday.

Materials needed...

Mirror. Tagboard.

Directions to students...

Touch your nose. You're touching the middle of your face, aren't you? Today, we are going to be thinking about that place below your hair and above your neck. Write your answers on your own paper.

1. How many parts of your face can you name? Look in the mirror to make sure you don't forget anything.

2. When someone's picture is in the newspaper, why is that person's face almost always shown?

3. When you talk to a person, what part of the face do you usually look at first?

4. Several things on your face come in pairs. What are they?

5. Look at yourself in the mirror. What part of your face is the closest to the mirror?

6. Look in the mirror and give yourself a big smile. How many teeth can you see?

7. Which parts of your face...
   a. move a little when you smile?
   b. don't move when you smile?

8. Frown at yourself in the mirror. Describe everything that happens to your face when you frown.

9. What is an eyelid?

10. Name two reasons why your eyelids are very important.

11. Why do you think people have eyelashes and eyebrows?

12. Put your fingers on your cheeks just in front of your ears. Then open and close your mouth a few times. Write a sentence about what you notice.

13. What are the two most important things you can't do without moving your jaw at least a little bit?

14. Where does the skin on your face stretch the most, and why do you think it stretches the most there?

15. You wear clothes on most of your body most of the time. Why don't you wear clothes on your face?

Bonus Question: You never think of a bird or a snake as having a face. Why not?

Comment...

Regarding Number 1, the dictionary will tell you that a face does not include the ears. However, you'll find many children will list their ears as part of their face — and why split hairs over that one? Just turn the other cheek!

Suggested answers...

1. eyes, nose, mouth, chin, eyebrows, eyelashes, eyelids, cheeks, jaw, lips, forehead; 2. because that is the part of the body which is easiest to recognize; 3. eyes; 4. eyebrows, eyes, eyelids, nostrils; 5. nose; 6. Answers will vary; 7. a. lips, cheeks, eyes (slightly), b. forehead; 8. Answers will vary; 9. A flap of skin that can cover the eye; 10. They shut out light when we sleep and they protect our eyes; 11. to keep small things from getting into our eyes; 12. I feel something moving (actually, it is the hinge of the jaw); 13. talk and eat; 14. the cheek area on either side of your mouth, so the mouth can open and close; 15. because we need to breathe, talk and see. *Bonus:* The word "face" is usually reserved for higher forms capable of facial expression. Birds and snakes seldom smile!

Snips

About this center...

This is a project in which the learning will take place by trial and error, so have plenty of paper squares available. When introducing this center, tell students that the outer edges of the squares may figure in the solutions. Also, be sure to reinforce the no-drawing rule.

Materials needed...

2″ × 2″ and 4″ × 4″ squares of white paper, scissors, and a wastebasket for scraps. Also, for the sign: tagboard, pair of school scissors, and string.

Directions to students...

To do your work today you will not be writing answers, you will be snipping them!

Here is an example. Think of a clown's hat. How can you use just two straight snips with the scissors to make the piece of paper have something to do with a clown's hat?

Here is one way to do it: Use two snips to make the hat.

Below is a list of words. Use one of the small pieces of paper for each word. Using the number of snips shown beside each word, try to do something to the paper to give us some idea about the word. If you make a mistake, it's okay to throw away the piece of paper and start over. Make all your snips straight — no curves — and you cannot draw on the paper before you start cutting.

Stairs (8 snips)

Stop sign (4 snips)

Butterfly (4 snips)

House (2 snips)

Now, using the larger squares of paper, snip away at these words. This time, you can use as many snips as you wish, but your snips must still be straight.

Fish

Star

Person

Comment...

If you want to make the second part of the activity more difficult, you could require that the fish be made with 8 snips, the star with 10 snips, and the person with 14 snips. (See illustrations.)

SNIP OUT AN INTERESTING
SHAPE FOR THIS CENTER.
YOU COULD USE A PAIR OF
REAL CHILDREN'S SCISSORS
FOR THE "SCISSORS BIRD"
SHOWN HERE...

POSSIBLE "SNIP" SOLUTIONS...

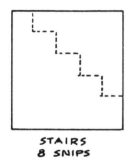

STAIRS
8 SNIPS

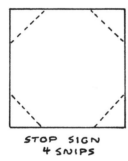

STOP SIGN
4 SNIPS

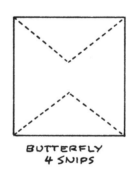

BUTTERFLY
4 SNIPS

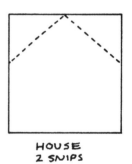

HOUSE
2 SNIPS

BONUS QUESTION POSSIBILITIES...

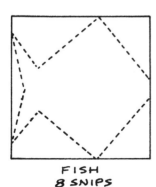

FISH
8 SNIPS

STAR
10 SNIPS

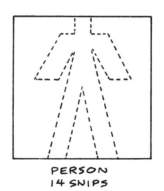

PERSON
14 SNIPS

If You Think of... (Part 2)

About this center...

This center reinforces the first "If You Think of" activity. We have included two of these simply because we think they are so much fun! Here, then, is more practice in original and flexible thinking.

Materials needed...

Nine note cards, tagboard.

Directions to students...

Number 1-16 on your own paper, look at the drawings, and then get ready for some fun thinking!

If you think of...

1. Number 5 as a yo-yo, what could Number 1 be?

2. Number 2 as a door, what could Number 3 be?

3. Number 4 as a bird, what could Number 9 be?

4. Number 8 as a frown, what could Number 4 be?

5. Number 7 as wind, what could Number 6 be?

6. Number 7 as cooked spaghetti, what could Number 1 be?

7. Number 5 as an egg yolk, what could Number 6 be?

8. Number 7 as thread, what could Number 1 be?

9. Number 2 as a chimney, what could Number 7 be?

10. Number 6 as popcorn, what could Number 9 be?

11. Number 5 as a city, what could Number 9 be?

12. Number 1 as a straw, what could Number 2 be?

13. Number 7 as noise, what could Number 1 be?

14. Number 3 as a stove, what could Number 9 be?

15. Number 8 as a rainbow, what could Number 5 be?

16. Number 5 as an eye, what could Number 8 be?

Comment...

We've thrown a couple of curveballs here. The suggested answer for Number 15 is "sun" because it takes sun to make a rainbow. However, "raindrop" would be an acceptable answer. Also, Number 13 is a question where the clue is totally conceptual. See how they handle it.

Suggested answers...

1. string; 2. window; 3. bug; 4. smile; 5. cloud; 6. uncooked spaghetti; 7. egg white; 8. needle; 9. smoke; 10. popcorn kernel; 11. town; 12. glass; 13. quiet; 14. pot or pan; 15. sun; 16. eyebrow.

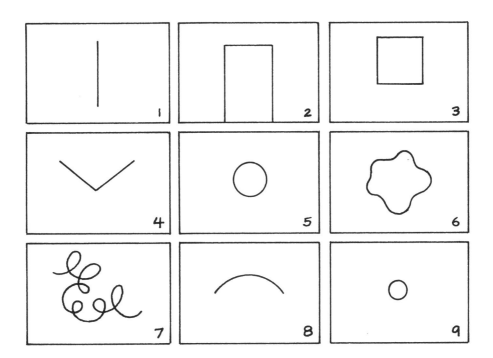

FOR INFORMATION ABOUT MAKING THIS CENTER,
SEE "IF YOU THINK OF... PART ONE (PG. 8)...

Stick Tricks

About this center...

The central idea here is to arrange all five sticks in some way that expresses the concept. Anyone could do this with 15 sticks, but the limitation imposed by the use of just five sticks assures that rigorous thinking must take place.

Materials needed...

Five popsicle sticks, pencil, drawing paper. Tagboard for sign.

Directions to students...

Your job is to use all five of the sticks to make a picture that looks something like each of the nine things listed below. You can put the sticks together in any way you wish, but you must use all five sticks each time. When you finish each stick picture, use a pencil to draw a little picture showing what you did.

Example:

This doesn't look exactly like a pine tree, but it looks something like one. It would be a good answer for the word, "tree."

Here are the words you are to work with:

Sign	Table	TV Antenna
Airplane	Hand	Person
House	Railroad Track	Hat

Comment...

Some children may be frustrated by the fact that their "pictures" don't really look like the objects in question. At this point, a brief discussion about picture symbols might be in order. Many street signs, signs at airports, etc. utilize this kind of symbolism. Also, be sure to let children know that the little drawings they make as "answers" do not have to be perfectly done.

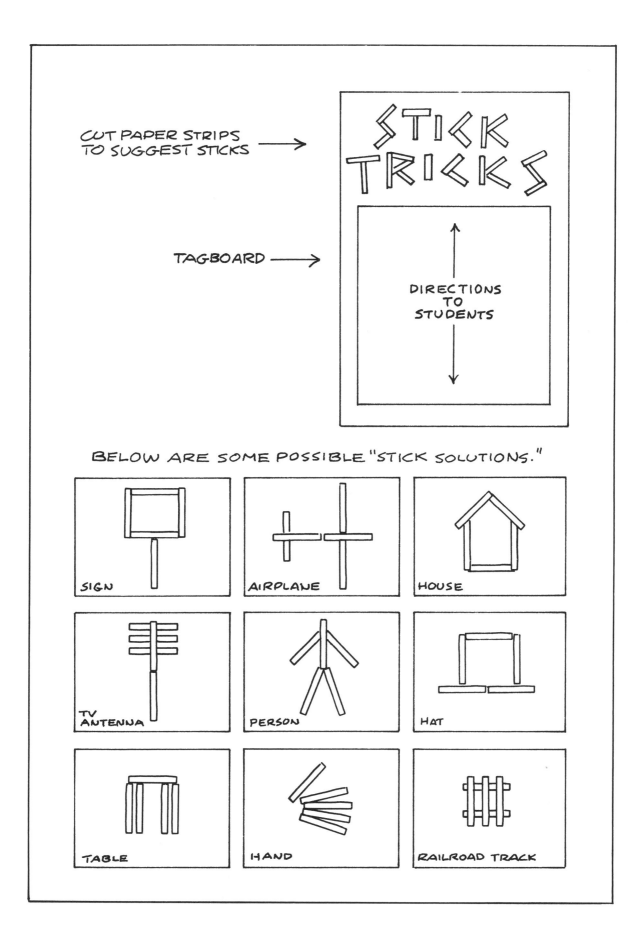

CUT PAPER STRIPS TO SUGGEST STICKS →

STICK TRICKS

TAGBOARD →

DIRECTIONS TO STUDENTS

BELOW ARE SOME POSSIBLE "STICK SOLUTIONS."

SIGN

AIRPLANE

HOUSE

TV ANTENNA

PERSON

HAT

TABLE

HAND

RAILROAD TRACK

Patterns

About this center...

There are many pattern activities available to students. What we hope distinguishes this one is the rapidly changing texture, which ought to keep children on their toes intellectually. Most of the inquiries involve sequential thinking, but several call for letter manipulation.

Materials needed...

Tagboard.

Directions to students...

Look at these patterns carefully. What do you need to add to finish them? Number your paper 1-15 and write (or draw) the missing letters, numbers or shapes that are needed to complete the pattern.

1. ooooooIoooooIoooooI_____

2. ⊡⊡⊡⊡ __

3. △▽I△▽▽I△▽▽▽I_____

4. oIooIoooIoooooIoooI____

5. ACB   JLK   RTS   L____

6. (Hear-He)   (Nose-No)   (Meat-Me)   (Soak_____)

7. (Best-State)   (Tenth-Thin)   (Into_____)

8. 2349   5679   1239   4_____

9. (Foot) (Ankle) (Knee) (Leg) (Waist) (Chest) (Neck) (_____)

10. ⬜⬜⬜ __

11. (An)   (Ban)   (Can)   (_____)

12. I ✛ ✳ __

13. (Look)   (School)   (Book)   (Stoop)   (W_____)

14. (Noon)   (Afternoon)   (Evening)   (Midnight)   (_____)

15. 154   253   352   _____ .

Comment...

Problems 6 and 7 are especially difficult, because students must get past the meaning of the words to analyze what is happening.

Suggested answers...

1. ○○○ 2. ⊡ 3. △▽ ▽ ▽ ▽ 4. ○○ 5. LNM; 6. So; 7. Took, Tooth, or Toad, etc. (word must begin with last two letters of previous word); 8. 569; 9. head; 10. ⬠ 11. Dan; 12. ✳
13. Wool or Wood; 14. Morning; 15. 451.

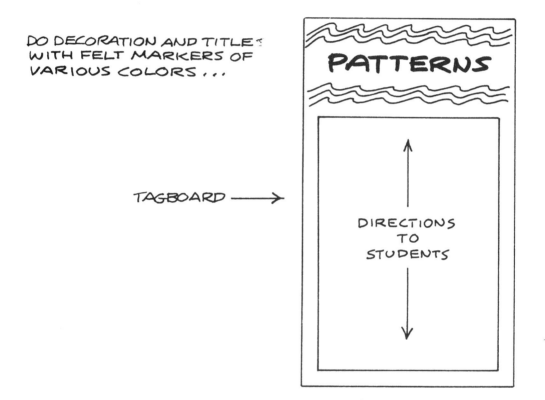

DO DECORATION AND TITLE
WITH FELT MARKERS OF
VARIOUS COLORS...

TAGBOARD ⟶

PATTERNS

DIRECTIONS
TO
STUDENTS

Who Says?

About this center...

This activity asks for youngsters to analyze certain situations based on their experience and to figure out who might be doing the talking. Brace yourself for the follow-up activity which focuses on Number 2!

Materials needed...

Tagboard.

Directions to students...

Below are some statements and questions. You must figure out who might be saying them. For example, if the question is, "Can you come out and play?" the answer would probably be, "a friend." Number 1-12 and do the work on your own paper.

1. Do you know how fast you were going?

2. Turn to page 51 in your book.

3. That will be three dollars and fifty cents.

4. How long until we get there?

5. Rain tonight with a chance of showers tomorrow.

6. Go to your room.

7. You're out!

8. Ham, cheese and a little mustard.

9. We will return after these messages.

10. I do.

11. Sit....now stay.

12. Sweetie pie, you look beautiful.

When you finish, think of how you answered Number 2 and then write five more sentences you think that person might say. If there is time, do the same for Numbers 6 and 11.

Comment...

Get ready for all the boys to groan when they get to Number 12.

Suggested answers...

1. policeman; 2. teacher; 3. sales clerk; 4. child; 5. weather person; 6. parent; 7. umpire; 8. customer; 9. TV announcer; 10. bride or bridegroom; 11. person talking to a dog; 12. boyfriend.

CUT QUESTION MARK FROM TAGBOARD OF A CONTRASTING COLOR AND GLUE IN PLACE. HAND LETTER THE TITLE AND DRAW "FACE."

TAGBOARD ⟶

WHO SAYS

DIRECTIONS TO STUDENTS

A Paper Problem

About this center...

With children getting more and more information passively from electronic sources, it is important that they have some experience with real objects. Each student will be working with a piece of waxed paper and a paper towel, so a trip to the grocery store is in order before you introduce this center.

Materials needed...

A segment from a roll of paper towels and a piece of waxed paper about the same size, magnifying glass, felt-tip pen with washable ink (for students to use at the center), pencil, white paper. Also, waxed paper, tape, tagboard for the sign.

Directions to students...

Do the work on your own paper.

1. List three ways in which the waxed paper is different from the paper towel.

2. Hold the waxed paper up to your cheek. Do the same thing with the paper towel. Which feels colder?

3. Shake the waxed paper and then shake the towel. Which makes the most noise?

4. Hold the towel up to your mouth and blow through it. Try to do the same thing with the waxed paper. Write a sentence about what you notice.

5. Write your name on a piece of white paper with the pencil. Put the waxed paper over your name. Then take the waxed paper away and put the towel over your name. Does your name show both times? Write a sentence about what you learn.

6. Tear a small piece from one corner of the towel and look at the torn place with the magnifying glass. Write a sentence about what you notice.

7. Tear a small piece from one corner of the waxed paper and look at the torn place with the magnifying glass. How is it different from the torn place on the towel?

8. Put the paper towel on the desk. Then press the point of the pen onto the towel. Hold it there while you count to 10. Write a sentence about what you notice.

9. Crumple the waxed paper into a tight ball and then spread it out and hold it up to the light. Write a sentence about what you notice.

10. Can you think of some things in nature that look something like the crumpled waxed paper when you hold it up to the light?

11. Crumple up the waxed paper again and smooth it out. Do the same thing 10 more times. What happens to the waxed paper?

12. Based on what you have just learned about the paper towel and the waxed paper, which would be better for:
    a. wrapping a sandwich?
    b. wiping up spilled milk?

Suggested answers...

1. thinner, smoother, not as soft, you can see through it more easily; 2. waxed paper; 3. waxed paper; 4. Air goes through the towel more easily; 5. You can read your name through the waxed paper but not through the towel; 6. There are many small threads (fibers); 7. The threads are smaller and there aren't as many; the torn place looks white; 8. The ink spreads out; 9. The paper is covered with many little lines (fold marks); 10. spider web, frost on a window, veins in a leaf, an elephant's skin; 11. It gets much softer; it makes very little noise; 12. a. waxed paper; b. paper towel.

Comment...

Regarding Number 8 — to avoid ink stains on a desk or tabletop, you may wish to put down a piece of cardboard to protect the surface.

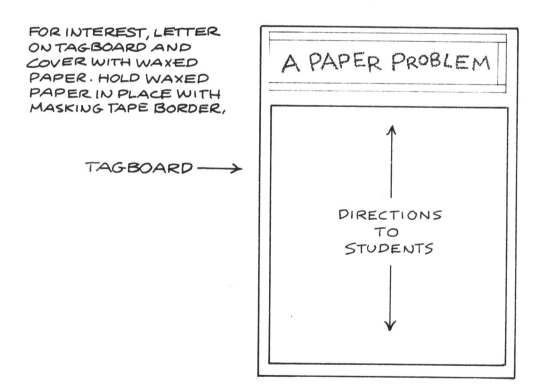

FOR INTEREST, LETTER ON TAGBOARD AND COVER WITH WAXED PAPER. HOLD WAXED PAPER IN PLACE WITH MASKING TAPE BORDER.

TAGBOARD ⟶

A PAPER PROBLEM

DIRECTIONS TO STUDENTS

Time to Eat

About this center...

The idea here is to encourage children to think carefully about the properties of foods in order to make appropriate responses. The assignment is made more difficult by requiring that the same answer cannot be used more than one time. Obviously, you may encounter "creative" spelling in some of the answers children supply, but if you get "pikull" instead of "pickle," give it its due!

Materials needed...

One pretzel, tagboard.

Directions to students...

Every answer will be the name of some kind of food, BUT — and here is the hard part — you may not use the name of a food more than once. Good luck! Write your answers on your own paper.

Name one thing you can eat that...

1. is square.

2. is shaped like a ball.

3. is shaped like a penny.

4. has to be peeled.

5. you eat everyday.

6. you never eat by itself.

7. is one color on the outside and another color on the inside.

8. turns your tongue a color.

9. is shaped like an icicle.

10. has one hole.

11. makes a lot of noise when it is heated.

12. has just one seed.

13. has many seeds.

14. is a seed.

15. comes in many small pieces.

16. is hard before it is cooked and soft after it is cooked.

17. is soft before it is cooked and hard (or at least pretty hard) after it is cooked.

18. usually comes in a box.

19. usually comes in a bag.

20. always comes in a wrapper.

21. you couldn't eat with a fork.

22. was made by an insect.

23. always comes in a jar.

24. is eaten on special occasions.

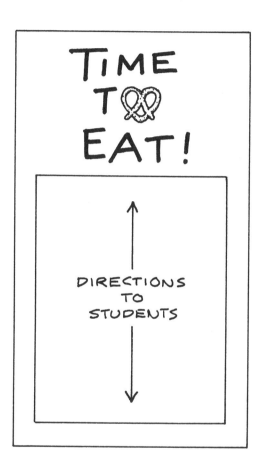

A PRETZEL FOR THE LETTER "O"... WHY NOT? IN FACT, YOU COULD USE PRETZEL STICKS FOR THE OTHER LETTERS IF YOU WISH. ATTACH TO TAG-BOARD WITH WHITE GLUE.

TIME T🥨 EAT!

DIRECTIONS TO STUDENTS

Comment...

You might wish to extend this activity by having paper plates and crayons available and having children draw their favorite dinner on the plates. (This is a good way to find out how many ways there are to draw tacos, hamburgers or pizza!)

Suggested answers...

1. cracker, some cookies, waffle; 2. plum, orange, grape; 3. pizza, some cookies, some crackers; 4. banana; 5. bread, probably cereal; 6. butter, flour, salt; 7. apple, watermelon, pink grapefruit; 8. popsicle, some candy; 9. carrot, ear of corn; 10. doughnut; 11. popcorn; 12. peach, plum, avocado; 13. watermelon, cantalope, tomato; 14. corn, pea, sunflower seed; 15. rice, macaroni, salt; 16. spaghetti, rice, carrot; 17. cake, cookie, some meat; 18. cracker, cereal, baking soda; 19. bread, potato chip, pretzel; 20. candy bar; 21. soup, stewed tomato; 22. honey; 23. pickle, ketchup, mustard; 24. turkey, cake, other foods depending on child's cultural background.

Stick Stories

About this center...

Children should be advised to look at all of the pictures and read all of the sentences before matching the components. Tell them to handle the easy ones first and then grapple with the more difficult ones through the process of elimination.

Materials needed...

12 note cards, tagboard.

Directions to students...

These sticks can do a lot of things! Match the 12 different things they are doing in the pictures with the things they are saying. Do the work on your own paper.

1. Hi, what's your name?

2. Boy, the wind is blowing hard.

3. This is as high as I can jump.

4. It feels good to be in bed.

5. I have a bad headache.

6. I like to ride in airplanes.

7. Push-ups are good for your arms.

8. Wow! My stomach aches!

9. Guess I'll sit down and have some breakfast.

10. Hey, come back here!

11. Maybe they won't see me hiding here in the corner.

12. Peek-a-boo!

Comment...

The interesting aspect of this center is the extreme simplicity of the drawings. So much can be suggested with so little!

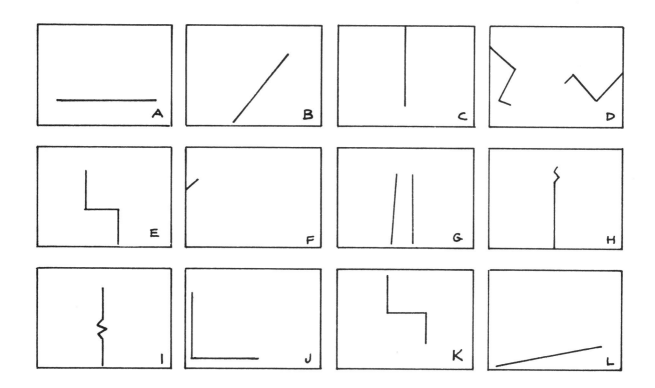

Suggested answers...

1. G
2. B
3. C
4. A
5. H
6. K
7. L
8. I
9. E
10. D
11. J
12. F

HAND LETTER TITLE. (OR YOU
COULD USE REAL STICKS OR
STRIPS OF COLORED PAPER.)

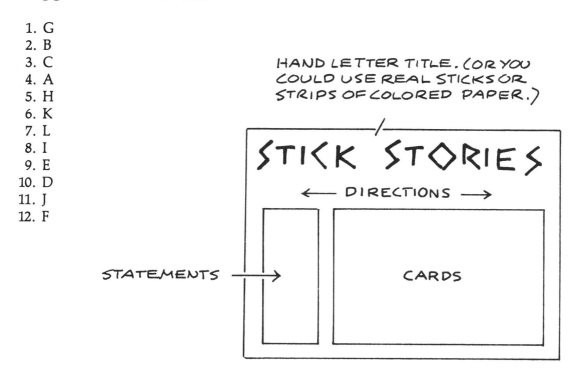

Adventures with Newspapers

About this center...

The intent here is simply to interest children in newspapers. Why? Because they are a valuable source of information...and learning.

Materials needed...

10 large note cards, magnifying glass, two different editions of the main news section of a newspaper (label one edition "A" and the other "B"). Tagboard for sign.

Directions to students...

Do you have a nose for the news? Let's find out! Do the work on your own paper.

1. Using the magnifying glass, look at a picture in one of the newspapers. Write a sentence about what you notice.

2. Write down everything that is the same about the front pages of both newspapers.

3. The headlines are the big, dark words above each story. Why do you think they are needed?

4. Using newspaper B, find the names of five people. Write them on your own paper.

5. Using Newspaper A, find the longest number on page 2. Write it on your own paper.

6. Using Newspaper B, find the word with the most letters on page 3. Write it on your own paper.

7. Using Newspaper A, find as many city names as you can on page 1. Write them on your own paper.

8. Hold one of the newspapers in one hand. Hold your answer paper in your other hand. Drop them both at the same time from the same height. Which landed on the floor first? Why?

9. Using the magnifying glass, look at the edges of the newspaper. Describe what you see.

10. Look at the front pages of both newspapers. Write down the second word in each headline. Then make up the longest sentence you can using every word on your list. You may add a few words of your own to help your sentence.

Comment...

Unfortunately, newspaper reading is no longer the strong daily habit it was for many people before the days of television. That's too bad. As educators (and as participants in a democratic system that needs an informed and involved citizenry), we should do what we can to encourage appreciation for the important contributions newspapers make.

Suggested answers...

1. I see many little dots; 2. (should include name of paper, same month and year, and other regular features which vary from paper to paper); 3. to tell us quickly what the story is about; 4. Answers will vary; 5. Answers will vary; 6. Answers will vary; 7. Answers will vary; 8. the newspaper, because it catches less air; 9. The top and bottom edges are jagged; 10. Answers will vary.

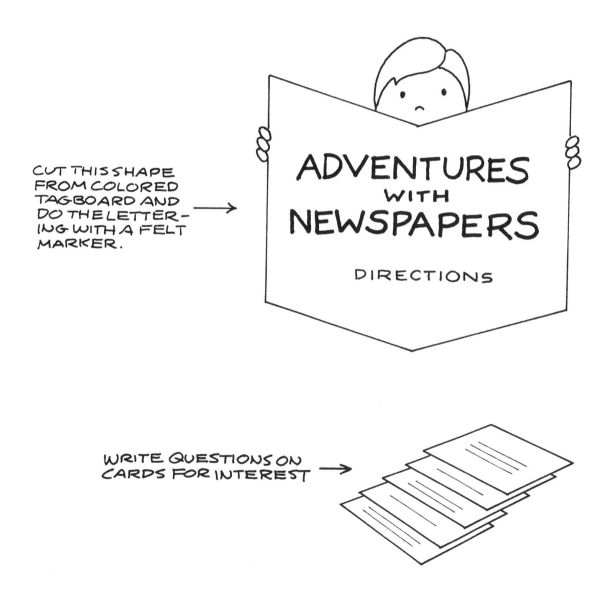

CUT THIS SHAPE FROM COLORED TAGBOARD AND DO THE LETTERING WITH A FELT MARKER. →

ADVENTURES
WITH
NEWSPAPERS

DIRECTIONS

WRITE QUESTIONS ON CARDS FOR INTEREST →

Why Not?

About this center...

Here, the effect is given and students must search for causes. The importance of this activity is that each problem must be approached in depth. Advise children to take their time, and stress that you are looking for an abundance of good answers.

Materials needed...

Tagboard.

Directions to students...

For this activity, you must think and think and think about each problem. For example, if you had to give reasons for why the sun might not be shining, you could say, "It might be night. It might be cloudy. There might be a thick fog. There could be an eclipse of the sun." Use your own paper to write your reasons.

1. Why might you not be able to see out a window?

2. Why might a plant not grow?

3. Why might a school not be open?

4. Why might a coat not look nice?

5. Why might a door not open?

6. Why might a house not be warm enough?

7. Why might you not get to talk to a person you want to call on the telephone?

Comment...

Don't accept answers which are totally "off the wall." For example, the answer that a door might not open because "it has been nailed shut" is too implausible. Or, if a student says a plant might not grow because "it has been put into a closet," point out that it also might not grow if it were planted on the moon! Remember, this is an analytical exercise, not an invitation to wild, imaginative excursions.

Suggested answers...

1. too dirty, shades down, curtains closed, steam has fogged the glass; 2. lack of water, too much water, lack of sun, too much sun, poor soil, too cold or hot, disease, pot too small, insect damage; 3. too early or late in the day, weekend, summer, other holidays, might be a problem with the furnace; 4. too large, too small, missing buttons, ripped, dirty, unattractive color; 5. locked, stuck; 6. furnace not working, very cold outside, not enough insulation, open windows or doors, walls have cracks; 7. person might not be home, might not hear phone, you might not know the number, might get wrong number, phone broken, phone lines down.

CUT SHAPES FROM TAG-BOARD. YOU MIGHT TRY HANGING THIS CENTER FOR ADDED INTEREST. →

DIRECTIONS TO STUDENTS

Snow and Pumpkins

About this center...

The challenge here is to think of the eight abstractions in one way and then to change gears in order to think of the same eight abstractions in a different way.

Materials needed...

Eight note cards, tagboard.

Directions to students...

All of these pictures have something to do with the weather. On a separate piece of paper, number 1-8. Then figure out which picture goes with each word, or words. (Use each picture only once.)

1. Rain

2. Wind and rain

3. Storm

4. Clear

5. Snow

6. Partly cloudy

7. Fog

8. Cloudy

Speaking of weather, the weather has something to do with gardens, doesn't it? Can you match the same pictures with what is being said about a garden? (Number 9-16 and keep going!)

9. I planted some seeds.

10. Things are really coming up now.

11. The ground is very dry.

12. What a great pumpkin patch!

13. I plowed the whole garden today.

14. The wind damaged my plants.

15. I finished half my work in the garden today.

16. Nothing has come up yet.

Comment...

As an extender, have students divide a piece of paper into four sections and then draw scenes which are sunny, foggy, rainy, stormy.

Suggested answers...

1. B
2. F
3. G
4. H
5. A
6. E
7. C
8. D
9. C
10. B
11. G
12. A
13. D
14. F
15. E
16. H

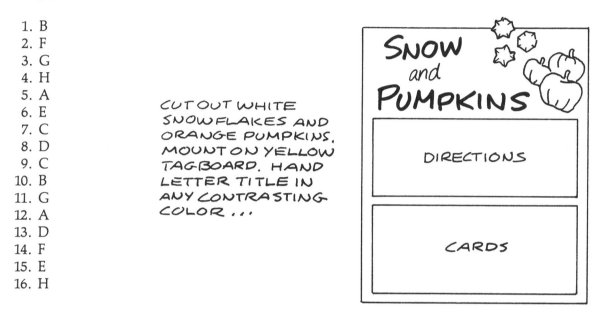

CUT OUT WHITE SNOWFLAKES AND ORANGE PUMPKINS. MOUNT ON YELLOW TAGBOARD. HAND LETTER TITLE IN ANY CONTRASTING COLOR ...

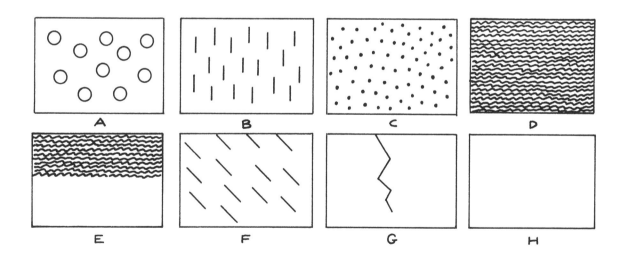

Good Luck 2 U!

About this center...

Here is a sprightly activity that invites children to play with language in a flexible, imaginative way. The emphasis is on how words sound, rather than on how they are spelled.

Materials needed...

Tagboard.

Directions to students...

Below is a list of letters. When you say them to yourself, you will find that they sound like words. Match the letters with the answers on the right. Do the work on your own paper. For example, the answer to Number 1 would be "G," something that flies.

1. B	A.	start of a question
2. M-T	B.	not me but...
3. K-T	C.	a vegetable
4. I	D.	not after but...
5. T-P	E.	something you drink
6. P-N-E	F.	like an ocean
7. I-C	G.	something that flies
8. C	H.	not full but...
9. L-O	I.	a flower
10. T	J.	not a town but a...
11. B-4	K.	a greeting
12. Y	L.	a person's name
13. U	M.	what roads are sometimes in the wintertime
14. P	N.	part of your face
15. C-T	O.	a kind of a tent

Comment...

We hope that children will be able to do this with a great deal of e-e-e-e-e's and that their i-i-i-i-i's will light up and that their brains will be b-z!

Suggested answers...

1. G
2. H
3. L
4. N
5. O
6. I
7. M
8. F
9. K
10. E
11. D
12. A
13. B
14. C
15. J

CUT THE LARGE "2U!" SHAPES FROM COLORED PAPER AND GLUE TO TAGBOARD...

Clue Cards

About this center...

The fun is in the flip-flop aspect of this activity. Students begin by looking at abstract clues in Part 1 to deduce the best match between cards and words. Their careful thinking about the first 10 challenges is rewarded by the 10 zany clues in Part 2, for which the cards are turned upside down.

Materials needed...

10 note cards, paper punch, scissors. Tagboard for sign.

Directions to students...

Part 1

Look at the cards and at the words below. Which card do you think has the most to do with each word? Number 1-10 on your own paper and match the letter on the card with the words. For example, Number 1 would probably be Card H, so you would write, "1-H."

1. Grass

2. Ball

3. Snow

4. Ocean

5. Planets

6. Sweater

7. Cat

8. Owl

9. Mouse

10. Smile

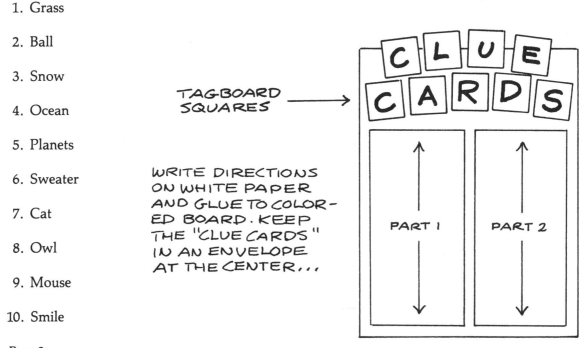

TAGBOARD SQUARES →

WRITE DIRECTIONS ON WHITE PAPER AND GLUE TO COLORED BOARD. KEEP THE "CLUE CARDS" IN AN ENVELOPE AT THE CENTER...

Part 2

Now number 11-20. Then turn the cards upside down and match the letter of the card (the letters will be upside down, too) with the crazy clues. Good luck!

11. Lizard's tongue

12. Bald-headed man

13. End of one piece of spaghetti

14. A piece of cheese bitten by an adult and child

15. A parade of very short people

16. Two balloons floating over a roof

17. A pan of cookies with some missing

18. Four turtles

19. A pair of short pants

20. A pair of short pants with pennies in the pockets

Comment...

There will be a few students who think in such literal terms that they may have trouble with this. On the other hand, it won't hurt them, and they just might start catching on...

Suggested answers...

1. H
2. J
3. D
4. B
5. E
6. F
7. I
8. A
9. C
10. G
11. C
12. G
13. J
14. E
15. H
16. I
17. D
18. B
19. F
20. A

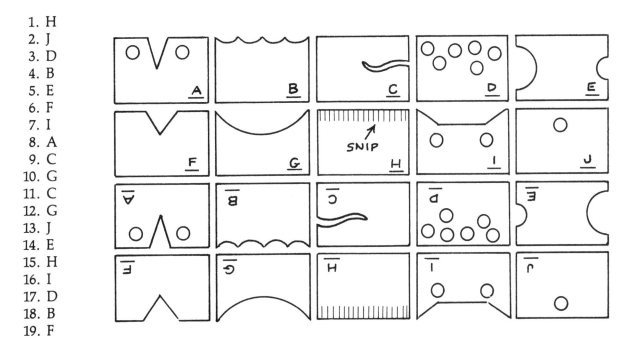

THE CARDS = RIGHT-SIDE-UP AND UPSIDE-DOWN. MAKE THEM WITH SCISSORS AND A PAPER PUNCH (FOR THE SMALL CIRCLES). THE LINES BENEATH THE LETTERS ARE NEEDED FOR THE "H" AND "I" CARDS.

Silly Questions About Simple Things

About this center...

It is important to emphasize that you want serious answers here. Although the questions are frivolous, the formulation of plausible responses will require some real mental agility.

Materials needed...

Tagboard.

Directions to students...

Even though these questions are silly, try to give the best, most important answer to each question. Do the work on your own paper.

1. Why don't you wash a car with a toothbrush?

2. Why don't people recycle used banana peels?

3. Why don't you wear shoes to bed?

4. Why don't you name all the ants in your yard?

5. Why don't people bring ladders to parades so they can see better?

6. Why don't people use popsicle sticks for toothpicks?

7. Why don't you cut grass with scissors?

8. Why don't you ride in an airplane to get to school faster?

9. Why don't tiny babies wear glasses?

10. Why don't you eat crackers with a fork?

Comment...

You'll have some fun with the answers to Question 8 because the reason is quite hard to express. Questions 2 and 4 are equally sophisticated. The concept of value and the impulse to give names are somewhat advanced, aren't they?

Suggested answers...

1. It would take too long; 2. Banana peels have no value; 3. You don't need to protect your feet in bed, and they would also get the bed dirty; 4. Names are generally given to people, pets, and things we care a lot about; 5. too clumsy and large to carry around; 6. The spaces between our teeth are too small for popsicle sticks; 7. would take too long and not do a very good job; 8. Airplane rides are for places quite far away, and schools are too close; 9. They don't read. Also, they might hurt themselves; 10. Crackers would crumble and it would be too messy.

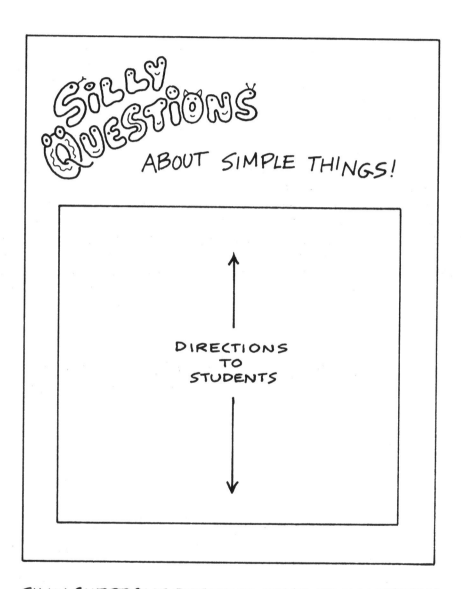

SILLY QUESTIONS DESERVE SOME SILLY LETTERS!
DRAW THE LETTERS DIRECTLY ON TAGBOARD WITH
COLORED MARKERS...

One Word, Please

About this center...

Not only will students have to analyze the various functions of the nouns in question, they will also have to be selective in choosing the best verbs to express the action of the nouns.

Materials needed...

Tagboard.

Directions to students...

Look at the list of nouns below. Your assignment is to find the best verb you can to describe something important about the action of the noun.

For example, you could use "croak," "jump," or "swim" for Number 1. Which do you think is the best? Or do you have a better idea?

Number from 1-20 on your own paper. Then write the words you see and add your own action words. What you will end up with are 20 very short sentences. Good luck!

1. Frogs _____.	11. Thunder _____.
2. Cows _____.	12. Clocks _____.
3. Snow _____.	13. Wind _____.
4. Snakes _____.	14. Eyes _____.
5. Spiders _____.	15. Babies _____.
6. Flowers _____.	16. Pitchers _____.
7. Wheels _____.	17. Motors _____.
8. Dogs _____.	18. Ice _____.
9. Bees _____.	19. Rivers _____.
10. Garbage _____.	20. Boats _____.

If there is time, write all the nouns on another piece of paper. Then look at your list of verbs and put them in different places to make some funny word-pairs. Example: Bees croak!

Comment...

Notice that the last few questions are a little more difficult. A variation of this activity would be for students to write every verb possible for each noun.

Suggested answers...

1. Frogs croak; 2. Cows moo; 3. Snow falls; 4. Snakes slither; 5. Spiders spin; 6. Flowers bloom; 7. Wheels turn; 8. Dogs bark; 9. Bees buzz; 10. Garbage smells; 11. Thunder booms; 12. Clocks tick; 13. Wind blows; 14. Eyes see; 15. Babies cry; 16. Pitchers pour; 17. Motors run; 18. Ice melts; 19. Rivers flow; 20. Boats float.

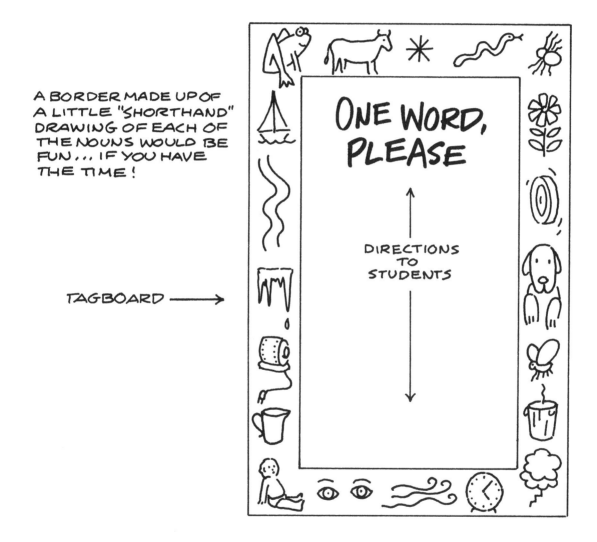

A BORDER MADE UP OF A LITTLE "SHORTHAND" DRAWING OF EACH OF THE NOUNS WOULD BE FUN... IF YOU HAVE THE TIME!

TAGBOARD ⟶

ONE WORD, PLEASE

↑

DIRECTIONS TO STUDENTS

↓

Blocks on Parade

About this center...

Some children may have difficulty with this project because it requires some conceptualization about elementary physical principles. The child who has spent hours playing with blocks will definitely have the edge in this one!

Materials needed...

Tagboard, six large note cards.

Directions to students...

Imagine that the squares in these six pictures are blocks. Look at the pictures carefully before writing your answers. To answer, write the letter of the picture, and then write a sentence telling why you answered as you did. (You won't need reasons for Numbers 7 and 8.)

1. Which would probably be the most fun to play on?

2. Which is most like a skyscraper?

3. Which is most like a train?

4. Which would not work if you tried to make it out of real blocks?

5. What would happen to the blocks in Picture C if you took away the top block?

6. Which looks most like a person?

7. Picture A is made of 10 blocks. How many more blocks would you need to make a pyramid one row taller?

8. What number do you get when you subtract the number of blocks in Picture F from the number of blocks in Picture D?

9. Pretend you could stand on top of the blocks in any of the pictures. Where would be the best place to be standing during an earthquake?

10. Look at Picture A. If you took away the bottom block on the left and the bottom block on the right, would the other blocks fall down?

Comment...

Who's to say for sure whether Picture E is the best "person?" If someone says that Picture B is a person standing up and Picture F is a person reclining...well, that's okay.

Suggested answers...

1. A — more climbing possibilities; 2. B — it is tall and thin and has many floors; 3. F — because the blocks look like train cars; 4. D — because there is nothing to hold up the blocks on the outside edges; 5. They would fall down because the top block holds the other blocks in place; 6. E — because it has a body and the top part looks like a head; 7. 5; 8. 4; 9. F — there is nothing above to fall on you, and you would not fall far if you fell off; 10. No — because the weight of the blocks on the top two rows would keep the three blocks in the third row in place.

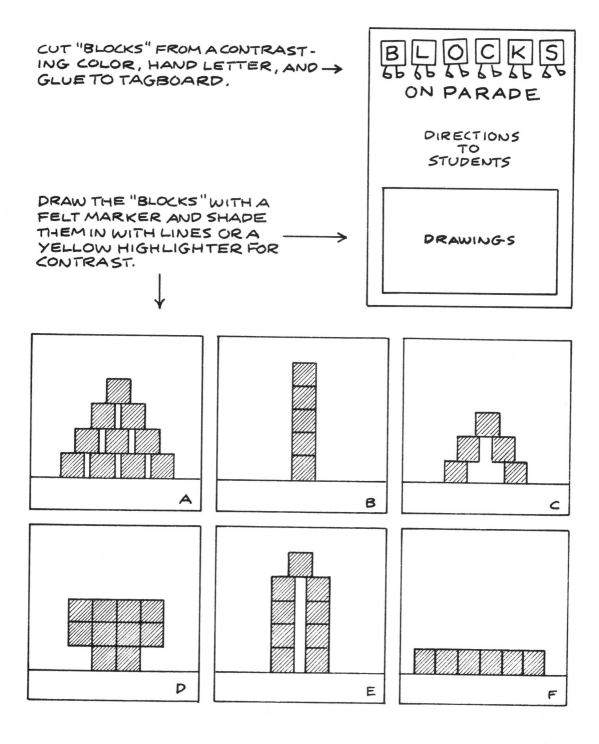

CUT "BLOCKS" FROM A CONTRAST- ING COLOR, HAND LETTER, AND → GLUE TO TAGBOARD.

DRAW THE "BLOCKS" WITH A FELT MARKER AND SHADE THEM IN WITH LINES OR A YELLOW HIGHLIGHTER FOR CONTRAST.

B L O C K S
ON PARADE

DIRECTIONS TO STUDENTS

DRAWINGS

A   B   C

D   E   F

Animal Whys

About this center...

This activity calls for careful thinking and common sense. The need for prior knowledge is minimal. Questions have been carefully chosen to give children an opportunity to draw logical conclusions — without having to go to an encyclopedia.

Materials needed...

Tagboard.

Directions to students...

Think carefully about these animal questions and write your answers on your own paper.

1. Why do polar bears have white fur?

2. Why do rabbits have big ears?

3. Why do turtles have shells?

4. Why do monkeys have fingers?

5. Why do cats have claws?

6. Why do giraffes have long necks?

7. Why do owls have big eyes?

8. Why do many bugs have green bodies?

9. Why do woodpeckers have long beaks?

10. Why do birds have hollow bones?

11. Why do ducks have webbed feet?

12. Why do skunks have a bad smell?

13. Why do frogs have eyes near the top of their heads?

14. Why do elephants have flat feet?

Comment...

It might be fun to bring everyone together at the end of this activity for a discussion about the various answers. If the conversation moves from turtle shells to porcupine quills, armadillo armor and toads that puff themselves up with air so snakes can't swallow them...hot dog!

Suggested answers...

1. to make them harder to see on snow and ice; 2. to help them hear their enemies; 3. so animals can't eat them; 4. to help them eat, climb, and swing; 5. to help them climb and hold their prey; 6. to eat leaves other animals can't reach; 7. to see when there is very little light; 8. to blend in with leaves and grass so their enemies can't see them; 9. to reach bugs in tree trunks and limbs; 10. to make them lightweight so they can fly; 11. to use as paddles in the water; 12. so their enemies will not want to attack them; 13. so they can see even when most of their body is underwater; 14. because they are so heavy.

DRAW THESE TALL BIRDS DIRECTLY ON TAGBOARD → WITH A FELT MARKER...

ANIMAL WHYS

QUESTIONS

Drawing in the Dark

About this center...

This is admittedly a gimmick, but it is a good way to encourage children to be thoughtful and flexible in their visual expression. The idea is simply to place a piece of paper inside the shoe box and have children reach in and draw on the paper without seeing what they are drawing. This is one center where you probably will need to explain the idea to the class first. Make sure you tell them you're not after great drawings, but rather "neat ideas," so under no circumstances are they to erase marks made "in the dark." Then, simply supply a set of cards with the instructions written on them. There are five possibilities suggested here. Perhaps you can think of others.

Materials needed...

A large shoe box, a supply of paper which has been cut to the dimensions of the bottom of the box, one "stubby" soft-leaded pencil (so children can draw with their hand inside the box without hitting the top of the box), five note cards, colored paper (for the sign on the top of the box).

Directions to students... *(to be presented on cards)*

- Start a drawing of a clown's head. Draw the shape of the head and two eyes and a nose. Then take the paper out of the box and finish your drawing in any way you wish.

- Draw a long line that has six wiggles and five loops. When you have done this, take your paper out and add more lines to make an interesting design.

- Draw a picture of yourself without looking at the paper until you are finished. Then take the paper out of the box and have a good laugh!

- Draw a picture of a tree, the moon, and six bats flying in the sky. Take the paper out of the box and complete your spooky picture in any way you wish.

- Draw a cat or dog without ever lifting your pencil from the paper while it is inside the box. In other words, your drawing will be just one long line. Then take the paper out and improve your drawing any way you like. Don't erase!

Comment...

The element of surprise adds to the effectiveness of this center. Students who are already good at expressing ideas visually will delight in this activity, but it should be a meaningful experience for all. (By the way, a man's shoe box or a boot box works best for this project, since an ample space gives youngsters greater freedom to draw.)

CENTER TITLE ON BOX LID.

DRAWING IN THE DARK

CUT OUT HAND HOLE

WRITE THE DRAWING ASSIGNMENTS ON CARDS

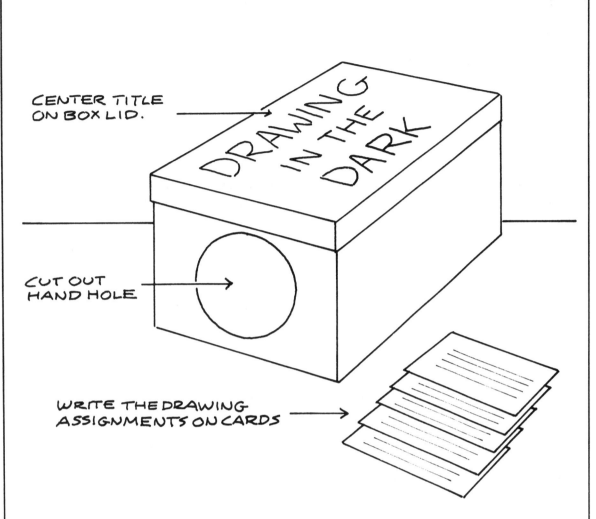

BELOW – SOME EXAMPLES OF "FINISHED" DRAWINGS.

 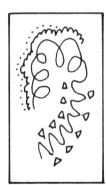   

A "DRAWING IN THE DARK" ART SHOW MIGHT BE FUN AS A CONCLUDING ACTIVITY.

Wacky Patterns

About this center...

This center has a strong element of frivolity, but actually children will need to do some careful reading and analytical thinking to provide acceptable answers.

Materials needed...

Tagboard.

Directions to students...

There is a pattern in each one of these silly sentences. Your job is to write a sentence telling what the pattern is. Also write down the number of words you find which help make the pattern.

1. Never go to school with toasters in your pocket unless you are willing to use an iron on handkerchiefs and stir soup in big pots and buy doughnuts with giant nickels held together with safety pins.

2. Polar bears carry salt in their paws for good luck and put snow in their milk when they aren't brushing their teeth in the bathroom to get ready for safety inspection.

3. Ages ago an alligator ate ants and angered auntie.

4. The house was filling up with towels and I hardly had room for my dresses and had to put the curtains in charge of keeping the bedspreads and shirts from getting mad at the carpet.

5. At breakfast, cooks do eggs for giant horses in jumpsuits.

6. If you roll a plate downhill when the moon is full and buttons are popping behind you, all the knobs on television sets will fall off and grapes and oranges will start singing.

7. Bats can hear ants as they sleep in groups while dogs skate on pies in the woods.

8. When the frog sat on a plate of peas, pine trees shivered, grass turned into lettuce, and parrots could be seen flying overhead with dollar bills in their beaks.

9. A flock of cardinals flew past six ladies lined up at the grocery story waiting to buy tomatoes, while their little boys munched happily on apples with ketchup in the middle.

Comment...

Children are natural humorists, and they find incongruities particularly amusing. We adults may have outgrown the ability to share in all the giggles, but at least we can make use of the motivational opportunity their wonderful *joie de vivre* offers!

Suggested answers...

1. metal things (5)
2. white things (5)
3. all words begin with "A" (9)
4. soft things (6)
5. first letters of words progress from "A" through "J" (10)
6. round things (6)
7. one-syllable words (17)
8. green things (7)
9. red things (4)

BEGIN WITH TAGBOARD AND THEN DO SOME SIMPLE LINE DRAWINGS SOMETHING LIKE THOSE SHOWN HERE. (NOTE THAT ALL OF THE DRAWINGS RELATE TO THE CENTER CONTENT.)

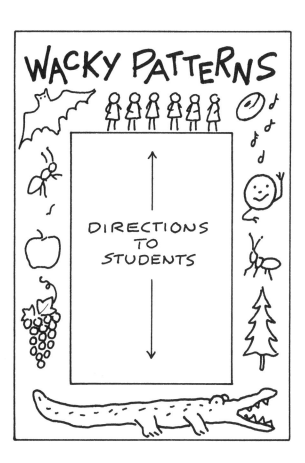

First Silly-bles

About this center...

This is good thinking practice. Students must replace the first syllable of each word with a word which fits both the rhyming pattern and the clue. When introducing the center, you may want to give students some examples of how the process works. Examples: An anteater without ants would be a "can't-eater." A buffalo that fights is a "tough-alo." A rhinoceros that knows the sum of 4 + 5 is a "nine-oceros."

Materials needed...

Tagboard.

Directions to students...

Today you are going to invent some new animals. How? By changing the first syllable of the animal's name so that it...

1. has something to do with the clue.
2. rhymes with the first syllable of the animal's real name.

Example: A crocodile that tells time is a.... "clock-odile!"

Number your paper 1-15 and write the word you invent.

1. A friendly alligator is a _____-igator.

2. An elephant that is healthy is a _____-ephant.

3. A hummingbird that is not smart is a _____-ingbird.

4. A turkey that is a girl is a _____-key.

5. A walrus that is not large is a _____-rus.

6. A honeybee that tells jokes is a _____-bee.

7. A zebra that unlocks doors is a _____-bra.

8. A badger that is very angry is a _____-ger.

9. A cardinal that is not near is a _____-dinal.

10. A catfish that is not skinny is a _____-fish.

11. A dinosaur that belongs to me is a _____-osaur.

12. A gorilla that has no money is a _____-illa.

13. A hippopotamus that takes very small drinks is a _____-opotamus.

14. A woodchuck that is not bad is a _____-chuck.

15. A kangaroo that likes firecrackers is a _____-aroo.

Comment...

If some children have trouble with this, suggest that they write out the first syllable of each word and mentally go through the alphabet for rhymes.

Suggested answers...

1. pal-igator; 2. well-ephant; 3. dumb-ingbird; 4. her-key; 5. small-rus; 6. funny-bee; 7. key-bra; 8. mad-ger; 9. far-dinal; 10. fat-fish; 11. mine-osaur; 12. poor-illa; 13. sip-opotamus; 14. good-chuck; 15. bang-aroo.

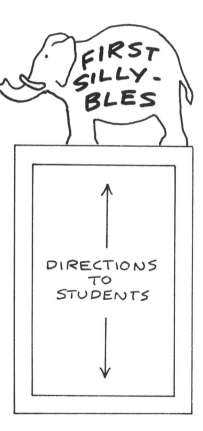

MAKE DISPLAY FROM TAGBOARD. YOU COULD VARY THIS BY USING A LARGE ANIMAL SHAPE FOR BOTH THE TITLE AND THE DIRECTIONS TO STUDENTS . . .

A String Thing

About this center...

It should come as something of a surprise to youngsters that an ordinary string has so many possibilities. Most of the inquiries which follow require close observation of the four strings in order to arrive at acceptable answers.

Materials needed...

Four soft strings 10 inches long, magnifying glass. One long string or piece of yarn for the tagboard presentation, tape.

Directions to students...

Now it is time for a fling with string! Do the work on your own paper.

Which string am I? (Answer with the number attached to the string.)

1. I'm like a ring or a pie.
   This is easy! What number am I?

2. I have something to do
   With seven minus two.

3. I could tie up a very small dog
   Or maybe catch the leg of a frog.

4. Someone as tall as two inches plus three
   Could have fun playing jump rope with me!

5. A ruler looks a little like me.
   Which number do you think I might be?

About string

6. Look at the end of one of the strings with the magnifying glass. Write a sentence about what you notice.

7. Use what you learned from Number 6 and write a sentence about how you think string is made.

8. What is the most important difference between string and thread?

9. What is the most important difference between string and wire?

10. Think of some way string is used...

   a. in a sport.
   b. as part of a toy.
   c. as part of something people wear.

Comment...

A magnifying glass is a magic tool for capturing a youngster's attention. It also promotes careful observation — and that's where original thinking frequently starts.

Suggested answers...

1. 2
2. 3
3. 4
4. 1
5. 3
6. I see many fuzzy threads.
7. It is made by twisting many little threads together.
8. String is thicker and stronger.
9. String is made of fibers and wire is made of metal.
10. a. basketball net, tennis net
    b. yo-yo string, kite string
    c. in some shoes and necklaces

THE "STRING THINGS" ARE SHOWN BELOW. TIE KNOTS AS SHOWN. WRITE NUMBERS ON ADHESIVE OR MASKING TAPE. ATTACH TO STRINGS.

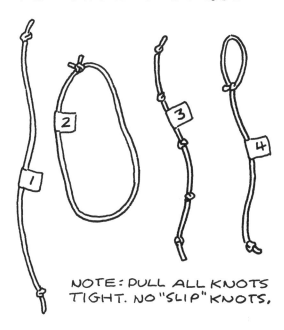

NOTE: PULL ALL KNOTS TIGHT. NO "SLIP" KNOTS.

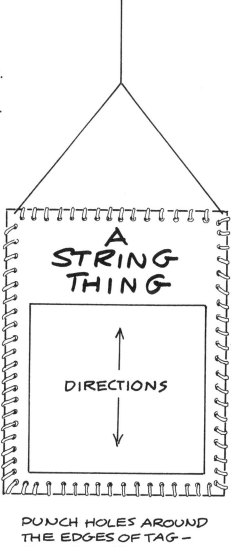

A STRING THING

DIRECTIONS

PUNCH HOLES AROUND THE EDGES OF TAG-BOARD DISPLAY AND LACE WITH YARN.

Senses

About this center...

In this activity, students are asked to think carefully about which senses they use in order to have knowledge about a particular concept. Caution them to work through the challenges slowly, asking themselves each time, "Do I see it, hear it, smell it, taste it, feel it?"

Materials needed...

Tagboard.

Directions to students...

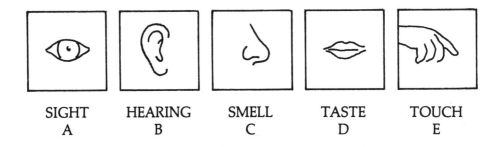

| SIGHT | HEARING | SMELL | TASTE | TOUCH |
| A | B | C | D | E |

What we know about things comes from our five senses...sight, hearing, smell, taste, and touch.

Below is a list of things you know something about. Number your paper 1-20. Then decide which sense was most important in helping you learn what you know about each thing. Which was the next to the most important? What should be in third place? Fourth? Fifth?

Use the letters you see under the pictures to show your answers. For example, if the subject were "robin," your answer might be — A, B. Why? Because you know how robins look and how they sound, but you don't know how they smell, taste or feel.

1. Pizza	6. Dog	11. Tree	16. Rain
2. Wind	7. Spider	12. Radio	17. Perfume
3. Book	8. Mud	13. Motorcycle	18. Popcorn
4. Rock	9. Rainbow	14. Kite	19. Ice
5. Carpet	10. Sweater	15. Soap	20. Television

Comment...

There are very few things that we experience through just one sense — and "rainbow" fits that category. At the other extreme is "popcorn," which involves all five senses. It should come as an interesting revelation to children that our perception of things usually calls for a variety of sensory input.

Suggested answers...

1. D, C, A, E
2. E, B
3. A, E
4. A, E
5. E, A
6. A, E, B, C
7. A, sometimes E — ugh
8. E, A
9. A
10. A, E
11. A, E
12. B, A, E
13. A, B, E
14. A, E
15. A, E, C, D
16. A, E, B, D
17. C, A, E
18. D, A, C, E, B
19. A, E, D, B
20. A, B, E

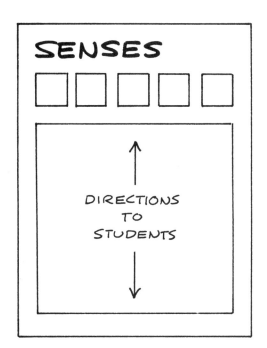

THE FIVE "SENSE" DRAWINGS SHOWN ON THE LEFT GO INTO THE BOXES SHOWN ABOVE. (NO NEED TO REPRODUCE THEM EXACTLY.)

A Date with States

About this center...

Students are asked to find words within words in this exercise. The use of state names simply adds interest and structure.

Materials needed....

Tagboard.

Directions to students...

The names of the states listed below will help you answer the questions, but be careful! In order to get the answers, you will have to look for little words hiding inside the bigger words. In some cases, you'll be looking for pieces of words that sound like real words. Good luck!

A. North Carolina   G. Mississippi

B. Montana   H. Illinois

C. Florida   I. Kentucky

D. Kansas   J. Oklahoma

E. Washington   K. Tennessee

F. Nebraska   L. Pennsylvania

1. Which state has something to do with being clean?

2. Which state has a part of it that sounds like something you walk on?

3. Which state has something to do with how you might drink water?

4. Which state has something to do with feeling sick?

5. Which state has something to do with what you write with?

6. Which state has something to do with what eyes do?

7. Which state has something to do with what you ride in?

8. Which other state has something to do with what you ride in?

9. Which state has a part which sounds like where you live?

10. Which state has something to do with what something weighs?

11. Which state has an ending which sounds like something used to open a door?

12. Which state has something to do with a color?

13. Which state has something to do with a girl's name?

14. Which state has something to do with a boy's name?

15. Which state has something to do with NOT hitting a ball?

16. Which state has something to do with a number?

17. Which state has two letters which mean "all right?"

18. Which state has a part which sounds like something that holds soup or corn?

19. Which state has something to do with what you do to get an answer?

20. Which state has a part that sounds like a mark made by a pencil?

Comment...

Why have children do this? Because hunts are fun, and the questions are designed to stimulate thinking. If your state is not included here, add it to the list and make up your own clue. Condolences, though, to New York — where clue-making seems just about impossible — unless children know enough zoology to be familiar with the gnu!

Answers...

1. E	11. I
2. C	12. B
3. G	13. A
4. H	14. I
5. L	15. G
6. K	16. K
7. A	17. J
8. L	18. D
9. J	19. F
10. E	20. A

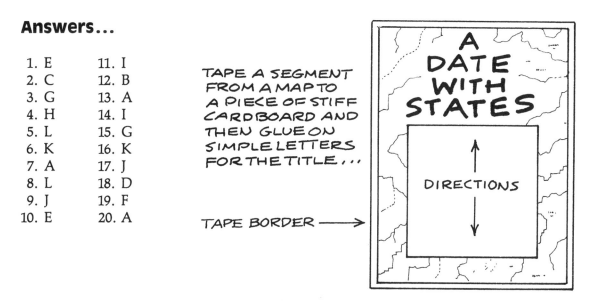

TAPE A SEGMENT FROM A MAP TO A PIECE OF STIFF CARDBOARD AND THEN GLUE ON SIMPLE LETTERS FOR THE TITLE...

TAPE BORDER ⟶

A DATE WITH STATES

DIRECTIONS

A Stick Is...

About this center...

In effect, this activity simply asks for definitions, and you should therefore encourage students to be as basic in their thinking as possible. Obviously, you're not going to get a lexicographer's definition. For example, the dictionary's first definition of "knob" is "a rounded protuberance." Chances are a youngster will say, "A knob is something you turn on a door." And that's okay...

Materials needed...

One stick about 10 inches long, tagboard.

Directions to students...

Number your paper 1-24 and finish these sentences in the best way you can. For example: Think about a stick. A stick sometimes has bark on it. You can hit a rock with it. It will break. But the most important thing you can say about a stick is that it is a small part of a tree that has broken away from the tree.

You should begin each sentence with the words below. One rule: You cannot use the main word more than once. You cannot say, "A wish is something you wish for." Good luck!

1. A knob is _____

2. A wheel is _____

3. A store is _____

4. A map is _____

5. A bunch is _____

6. A table is _____

7. A bubble is _____

8. A ring is _____

9. A wish is _____

10. A stamp is _____

11. A frown is _____

12. A friend is _____

13. A speck is _____

14. A pet is _____

15. A nail is _____

16. A comb is _____

17. A question is _____

18. A wall is _____

19. A sentence is _____

20. A poem is _____

21. A nap is _____

22. A knee is _____

23. A tooth is _____

24. A dent is _____

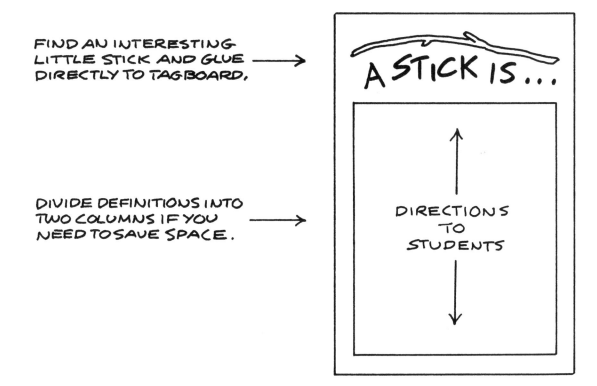

FIND AN INTERESTING LITTLE STICK AND GLUE DIRECTLY TO TAGBOARD. →

DIVIDE DEFINITIONS INTO TWO COLUMNS IF YOU NEED TO SAVE SPACE. →

A STICK IS...

DIRECTIONS TO STUDENTS

Comment...

This may be frustrating to some children because they may lack the vocabulary and experience to provide really fundamental definitions. Nevertheless, in most cases they should be able to provide an acceptable answer.

And oh, if a student says a table is a "rigid plane held parallel to the floor at a convenient height by four vertical shafts," immediately allow that child to take over your class!

Suggested answers...

Answers will vary. You are the best judge as to whether students are doing work which reflects their real abilities.

Spots and Dots

About this center...

Very simple, open-ended clues will spur some imaginative writing in this activity. Students look at the picture, begin their stories with the two or three words given, and are then free to take off in any direction they choose!

Materials needed...

Six large note cards, tagboard.

Directions to students...

What's happening to these spots and dots? Look at each picture. Then, on your own paper, write a short story which begins with the words you see next to each picture. Your story must be at least four sentences long.

Here is an example to give you the idea. WE WENT to the lake and walked all of the way around it. Ten of us went, so there would be plenty of eyes to see what would come out of the water. We waited and waited. Then a big green thing appeared!

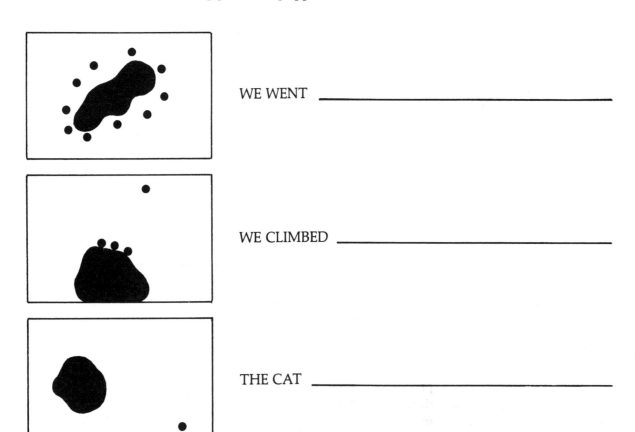

WE WENT _____

WE CLIMBED _____

THE CAT _____

WE LOOKED UP _____

THE BIRDS _____

A LITTLE ANT _____

MOUNT THE SIX DRAWINGS ON A
VERTICAL PIECE OF TAGBOARD. →
HAND LETTER THE TITLE...

SPOTS
AND DOTS

DIRECTIONS

Comment...

Less is sometimes more! By keeping the information simple, you stimulate the imagination. For example, it can be argued that a story in a book (or a drama on radio) can be more compelling than a television show or a movie simply because the imagination is free to play a greater role. (Your students won't buy that line of reasoning, of course, but the principle is valid nevertheless.)

Tube Talk

About this center...

A paper tube is something which is usually thrown away without much thought. In this context, however, the lowly tube takes center stage as students are asked a wide-ranging series of questions. This is a good hands-on project, guaranteed to elicit some surprising reactions. Regarding Question 5, the dot is important because it is impossible to determine how many times the tube revolves without some point of reference.

Materials needed...

A tube from a roll of paper towels, a pencil, a rectangular rubber eraser, an 18″ piece of string (thin enough to hang straight), a ruler. For the sign, a second tube, string and tagboard.

Directions to students...

Do the work on your own paper.

1. A straw is a tube but a pencil is not. Why?

2. Think of a flower. Which part of a flower is something like a tube?

3. What do you call a tube that...
    a. carries water to a house?
    b. carries blood through your body?
    c. carries smoke out of a house or building?

4. The tube you are working with held paper towels. How do you think the towels were attached to the tube?

5. Put the tube on the left edge of your desk (or table) and roll it slowly to the right edge. How many times does it go around to get all the way across? (*Hint:* Find the dot and let it help you.)

6. Put the pencil inside the tube and roll the tube slowly.
    a. What happens to the pencil?
    b. How well does the tube roll?

7. Put the eraser inside the tube and roll the tube slowly.
    a. What happens to the eraser?
    b. How well does the tube roll?

8. Put the tube up to your ear and listen. Write a sentence about what you hear.

9. If you took the tube apart, what would the piece of cardboard it is made from look like? Write your answer.

10. Point the tube toward a window or a light and peek into the end. Draw a little picture of the pattern you see inside the tube.

11. About how far in inches is it around the tube? (*Hint:* Use the string.)

12. What is the easiest way to thread the string through the tube? Write your answer.

Comment...

No need to get into physics or solid geometry here! Obviously, there are fundamental mechanical principles at work in some of these activities, but the point here is chiefly to stimulate curiosity. The time will come when they will see the similarity between the construction of the tube and the principle of Archimedes' screw.

Suggested answers...

1. The straw is hollow and the pencil is not; 2. stem; 3. a. pipe, b. vein, c. chimney; 4. glued (slight glue marks should be visible); 5. Answers will vary; 6. a. It stays on the bottom and rolls, b. pretty well; 7. a. It goes part way up and then falls down, b. not very well; 8. I hear a swishing sound; 9. It would be long and skinny; 10. (Note: student should observe a spiral pattern); 11. usually about 5½ inches; 12. Hold the string up so it hangs straight and lower it down through a tube which is held vertically.

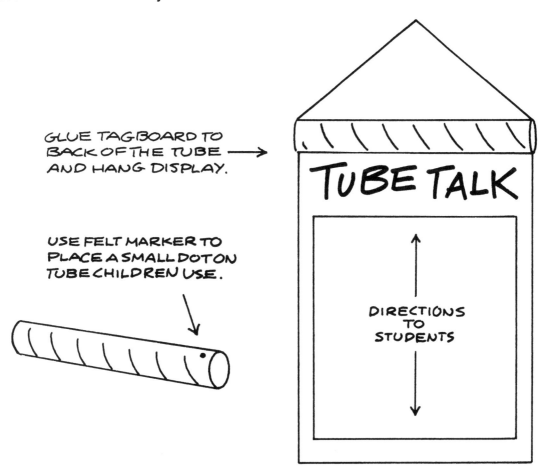

GLUE TAGBOARD TO BACK OF THE TUBE AND HANG DISPLAY. →

USE FELT MARKER TO PLACE A SMALL DOT ON TUBE CHILDREN USE.

TUBE TALK

DIRECTIONS TO STUDENTS

Good Night

About this center...

These questions about sleep ought to keep youngsters wide awake as they think about a familiar activity in a variety of interesting ways.

Materials needed...

Tagboard.

Directions to students...

Write your answers on your own paper.

1. Why do you sleep?

2. How can you tell when someone else is asleep?

3. Why do most people like to sleep in the dark?

4. Why does your hair get messed up when you sleep?

5. Why do most people sleep with their heads on pillows?

6. Why do you change clothes when you sleep?

7. Why are most beds shaped like rectangles?

8. Besides beds, what other things are found in most bedrooms?

9. Do people think when they sleep? Explain.

10. Quite a few animals are awake at night and sleep in the day. Can you name some?

11. Some people have jobs at night and sleep during the day. What kinds of jobs do they do?

12. What are some of the signs that show someone needs sleep?

13. Do you ever have trouble getting to sleep? Why?

14. As you are going to sleep at night, what sounds do you hear?

15. It is always bedtime for someone somewhere in the world. Explain.

Comment...

You'll notice we have avoided nightmares, things under the bed, etc. We've also steered clear of teddy bears and other security symbols children might want to keep private.

Suggested answers...

1. I sleep because my body needs rest each day; 2. Their eyes are closed and they don't know what is going on around them; 3. Our eyelids do not completely shut out the dark and so we like to make the room dark; 4. I toss and turn many times as I sleep; 5. They are soft, and they hold my head even with the rest of my body; 6. Daytime clothes would get wrinkled and also would not be very comfortable; 7. Because our bodies fit comfortably on that shape; 8. night lights, reading lights, mirrors, closets, chests, curtains, carpet, hangers, shoes, clothes, night stands; 9. Yes, we experience thoughts and feelings in the form of dreams; 10. skunks, bats, opposums, raccoons, porcupines and many others; 11. cab drivers, policemen, firemen, doctors, nurses, bus drivers, bakers, pilots, janitors, newspaper workers, train workers, some mail workers; 12. They yawn, their eyes get droopy, they aren't as alert, they have dark circles under their eyes, they are grouchy sometimes; 13. Answers will vary; 14. Answers will vary; 15. Since the world turns, it is always night somewhere.

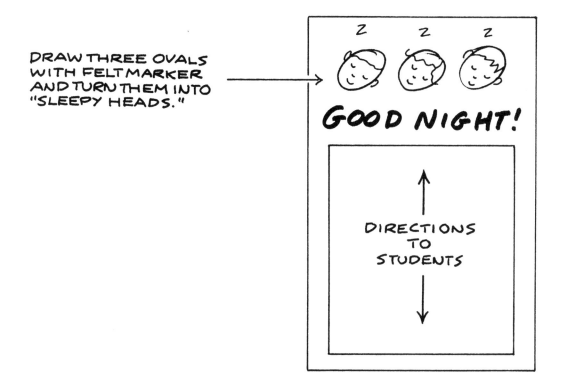

Index

Other Publications by Tin Man Press

Nifty Fifty — 500 thinking challenges about 50 familiar things.

Is It Friday Already? Learning Centers That Work — A year's worth of learning center ideas in nine subject areas.

The Great Unbored Bulletin Board Book — 20 challenging bulletin board ideas you've never seen before.

The Great Unbored Bulletin Board Book II — Who says sequels can't be equal? This one is. 20 more original boards.

The Great Unbored Blackboard Book — Uses the blackboard as a focus for lively thinking activities.

Waiting for Lunch — Serves up quick, easy, mostly oral activities to do with your class when you have an extra few minutes.

OPQ — Offbeat Adventures with the Alphabet — The alphabet becomes the springboard for all sorts of intellectual play.

Linework — A 64-card set designed to give children varied and unusual experiences with the concept of line.

An Alphabet You've Never Met — This 64-card set asks students to think of words suggested by some creative tampering with letters.

Discover! — A series of 24 card sets which use everyday objects for a hands-on approach to thinking skills. 20 challenges per set.